Knowing Our Catholic Faith

Beliefs and Traditions Worktext

Level Four

Loyola Press

The Ad Hoc Committee to Oversee the Use of the Catechism, National Conference of Catholic Bishops, has found this catechetical series, copyright 2000, to be in conformity with the *Catechism of the Catholic Church.*

Nihil Obstat: Michael Cameron, Ph.D.
                 Censor Deputatus
                 March 21, 1999

Imprimatur: Most Reverend Raymond E. Goedert, M.A., S.T.L., J.C.L.
                Vicar General
                Archdiocese of Chicago

Given at Chicago, Illinois, on March 25, 1999.

The *Nihil Obstat* and *Imprimatur* are official declarations that a book or pamphlet is free of doctrinal or moral error. No implication is contained therein that those who have granted the *Nihil Obstat* and *Imprimatur* agree with the content, opinions, or statements expressed.

Acknowledgments: The Scripture quotations contained herein are from the *New Revised Standard Version Bible*, copyright © 1989 by the Division of Christian Education of the National Council of the Churches of Christ in the U.S.A., and are used by permission. All rights reserved.

English translation of the Act of Contrition from the *Rite of Penance* © 1974, International Committee on English in the Liturgy, Inc. (ICEL); the English translation of Come, Holy Spirit from *A Book of Prayers* © 1982, ICEL. All rights reserved.

English translation of the *Catechism of the Catholic Church* for the United States of America copyright © 1994, United States Catholic Conference, Inc.—Libreria Editrice Vaticana.

English translation of the Lord's Prayer and Apostles' Creed by the International Consultation on English Texts (1975).

(Acknowledgments continued on the inside back cover.)

Editors: Amy Joyce, Anna Urosevich, Pedro Vélez

Cover Design: Jennifer Carney

Production: Genevieve Kelley, Molly O'Halloran, Jill Smith, Leslie Uriss

ISBN: 0–8294–1132–1

3441 North Ashland Avenue
Chicago, Illinois 60657
1-800-621-1008

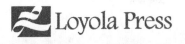 Loyola Press

00 01 02 03 04 5 4 3 2

Knowing Our Catholic Faith

Beliefs and Traditions Worktext

Level Four

Author

Peg Bowman

Contributing Author

Mary K. Yager

Principal Program Consultants

Sister Kathryn Ann Connelly, S.C.

Most Reverend Sylvester D. Ryan, D.D.

Reverend Richard Walsh

Jacquelyne M. Witter

 Loyola Press

Contents

My name is _____.

I am a member of the Catholic Church.

My Parish is _____

in _____.

This book will teach you some important and interesting things about the Catholic **faith**. You will read about what we Catholics believe, how we celebrate, how we live our faith, and how we pray. The facts and ideas in this book are taken from a much larger book called the *Catechism of the Catholic Church*. Use this worktext to learn more about being a member of the Catholic Church.

The activities will help you remember the things you learn. Sometimes you will review Catholic beliefs, traditions, and practices you already know. There will be new facts and ideas in this book, too. You will learn some new words and terms and meet some great saints. You will also learn some new prayers.

Our Catholic Beliefs

Whether you have been a Catholic all your life, or are a new member of the Church, you probably have thought a lot about God and already know many important things about God. As a member of the Catholic Church, you want to know as much as you can of what we Catholics believe about God the Father, Jesus his Son, and the Holy Spirit.

These lessons and activities will also teach you more about our Blessed Mother, Mary, about some people of the Old Testament, and about some of the great saints of the Church.

One God, Three Persons

Catechism paragraphs 199–202, 222–267

We believe in one God. Sometimes you might hear about people who believed in many gods. They thought different gods had different jobs to do or watched over different things on earth.

God has revealed that he is one. We read in the **Old Testament** in the **Bible,** "The Lord is our God, the Lord alone" (Deuteronomy 6:4). In the **New Testament,** Jesus himself tells us "the Lord is one" (Mark 12:29). There are not many gods, but only one, true God.

It is a **mystery of faith** that God is one. We cannot understand all there is to know about God, but we can believe by using our gift of faith.

There are three persons in one God. Now we come to the greatest mystery of faith. It is the mystery of the **Holy Trinity.** The Holy Trinity is the name we use to talk about the three persons in one God. The three persons of the Holy Trinity are God the **Father,** God the **Son,** and God the **Holy Spirit.**

Remember! There is only one God. God the Father is God. God the Son is God. God the Holy Spirit is God.

There is one God. There are three persons in one God. Each person is not a separate God. There is only one God.

We cannot understand how there can be three persons, but only one God. God has revealed this to us. Our faith tells us this is true.

Know Our Catholic Tradition

Meet a great Catholic saint. Saint Augustine was one of the greatest teachers who ever spoke and wrote about God. But he did not always believe in God! He became a believer because his mother, Saint Monica, prayed for him. He learned about the Catholic faith from a great teacher, Saint Anselm. After he was baptized, Augustine wrote many sermons and books about God. One of his most famous sayings is: "You have made us, O God, for yourself, and our hearts shall find no rest until they rest in you."

Clues and Transfers

Fill in each blank below to spell correct answers. When a line has a number beneath it, transfer that letter to the blank marked with that number at the bottom of the page. When you are finished, the transfers will spell a mystery of faith.

1. We believe in God by using our ___ ___ ___ ___ of faith.

11   1

2. The Holy Trinity is the greatest mystery of ___ ___ ___ ___ ___ .

6   2

3. The mystery of the Holy Trinity means there are

   ___ ___ ___ ___ ___ ___ ___ ___ ___ ___ ___

3   10   5   4   9   7

in one God.

4. The Third Person of the Holy Trinity is ___ ___ ___ the

8   13

   ___ ___ ___ ___ Spirit.

12

A MYSTERY OF FAITH:

___ ___ ___ ___ ___ ___ ___ ___ ___ ___ ___ ___ ___

1   2   3   4   5   6   7   8   9   10   11   12   13

Catechism paragraphs 279–301, 315, 317, 328–336, 350, 355–373, 381–383

Go outside and look around you. What do you see? Can you see the sky? Are there trees? Grass? Flowers or plants? Can you see or hear any birds? Go out at night and look at the stars. Is the moon in the sky tonight? What can you hear? What can you smell?

There is nothing you can see, hear, touch, or smell that God didn't **create!** If it weren't for God, there would be *nothing!*

No one really knows *how* God created the world and everything in it. It is another mystery that God *always was.* Everything else in the world came to be because God created it. God created everything *out of nothing!*

God also created beings we cannot see. We call them **angels.** Angels are spirits; they do not have bodies. They live in heaven with God, where they praise him and serve him. Sometimes God uses the angels as messengers to people on earth. God also has given each of us a guardian angel to watch over us.

When God created us, he gave each person a body that can be seen and heard and touched, and a **soul** that cannot be seen.

God created human beings *in his own image.* He created us to have both a body that will die and a soul that will live forever. God created us human beings to live with him forever.

Know Our Catholic Belief

The Book of Tobit in the Old Testament tells about the angel Raphael. Raphael helped a young man named Tobiah through many adventures on a long journey. Many people still pray to the angel Raphael today to keep them safe when they travel.

My Favorite Things God Created

In each box below, draw some of your favorite things that God created.

My favorite people

My favorite animals

My favorite flowers and plants

My favorite outdoor scene

My favorite kinds of weather

A Fall and a Promise

Catechism paragraphs 374–405, 412

When God created angels and human beings, he gave them each *free will.* This means that angels and human beings are free to choose what they will do. We can choose whether we will do the right thing or the wrong thing.

Most of the angels used their free will to choose the right thing. But some of the angels chose to reject God. They had to leave heaven. Their leader was an angel called Satan. Satan and the other bad angels live in hell.

In the Book of Genesis, the first book in the Old Testament in the Bible, we can read about the first man, Adam, and the first woman, Eve. God created them in his own image and placed them in a beautiful garden called Eden. The story tells us that Adam and Eve were perfectly happy there. They had everything they needed and they could walk and talk with God every day. They knew God was their creator and that they owed everything to God.

Then, Satan came to the first humans. The Bible tells us Satan tempted them to eat some fruit from a tree that God had said they could not touch. Satan told Adam and Eve they could be as great as God. He said they did not need to **obey** God.

This was the first time human beings used their free will to choose to do the wrong thing. This wrong choice was a serious sin. We call the sin of Adam and Eve **original sin.**

Original sin did not end with Adam and Eve! Because of their bad choice, God made them leave Eden. They now had to work to have the things they needed. They were no longer perfectly happy. They could not walk and talk with God. Worst of all, the gates of heaven were locked. And they passed this state of sadness and sin on to all their children. They passed it on to *each human being.* We are all born with original sin on our souls.

But God gave Adam and Eve great hope. God promised that someday he would send a **Savior.** The Savior would free human beings from original sin and would unlock the gates of heaven.

Know Our Catholic Belief

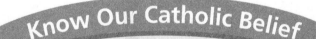

Jesus set us free from original sin when he died and rose from the dead. **Baptism** is the sacrament that removes original sin from our souls.

An A–maze–ing Message

As Adam and Eve left the Garden of Eden, God gave them a message of hope. Follow Adam and Eve out of the garden through the maze below. When you follow the maze correctly, you will read God's message of hope. After you have made it through the maze, transfer the letters of God's message to the space below.

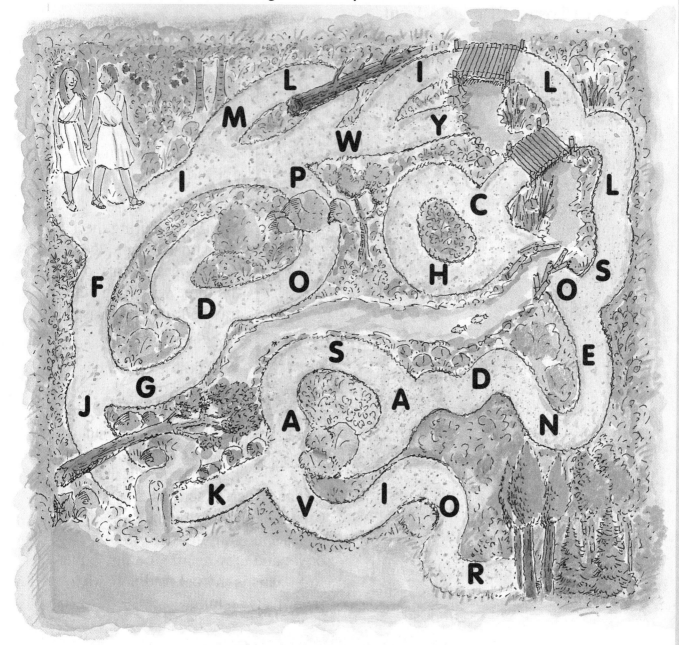

THE MESSAGE: __ __ __ __ __ __ __ __

__ __ __ __ __ __ __.

The Promised One

Catechism paragraphs 512–537, 561, 1194

Each year, we celebrate a season called Advent for the four weeks before Christmas. During **Advent,** we remember how the people of Israel waited thousands of years for a Savior. We remember how Mary and her husband, Joseph, waited for Jesus to be born. Like them, we now wait for the coming of Jesus.

The Son of God came to us as a little baby! We celebrate the birth of Jesus on December 25, *Christmas day.* But our celebration doesn't stop there! The Christmas season includes four Sundays after Christmas as we recall the stories about Jesus when he was a baby, a young boy, and a young man.

You can read the stories in the **Gospels** of Matthew and Luke in the New Testament. They tell us Jesus was born in Bethlehem while Mary and Joseph were visiting there.

On the *Feast of the **Holy Family,*** the Sunday after Christmas, we learn how Jesus lived and grew up at home with Mary and Joseph. He loved them and learned from them and obeyed them.

On the *Feast of the **Epiphany,*** during the Christmas season, we remember the story of the three wise men who traveled from the East to see Jesus.

We end the Christmas season with the *Feast of the Baptism of the Lord.* He was a young man when John the Baptist baptized him in the Jordan River. When Jesus was baptized, people saw the Holy Spirit come upon him in the form of a dove, and they heard God the Father say, "This is my beloved Son. My favor rests on him."

Know Our Catholic Tradition

The word *Emmanuel* means God-with-us. It is a name we use for Jesus. During Advent, we pray and sing, "O come, O come, Emmanuel."

Hidden Message Crossword

Complete the crossword puzzle. Then, unscramble the letters that are in circles to complete the hidden message at the bottom of the page.

Across

2. Feast when the three wise men came to see Jesus.
4. Jesus grew up in a _____ with Mary and Joseph.
6. Feast of the birth of Jesus.
7. God the Father called Jesus his _____ Son.
8. At his Baptism, the Holy Spirit came upon Jesus in the form of a _____.
9. At the end of the Christmas season, we celebrate Jesus' _____.

Down

1. The people of Israel waited _____ of years for a Savior.
3. We read stories of Jesus' early years in the _____ of Matthew and Luke.
5. The season when we wait for the coming of Jesus.

THE HIDDEN MESSAGE:

Jesus is God the Father's ___ ___ ___ ___ ___ ___ ___

After Jesus was baptized, he went out to the desert to be alone and pray. He stayed there forty days and at the end of that time, he was tired and hungry. Satan came to Jesus then and tried to tempt him to turn away from God. He tried three different temptations, but each time, Jesus said "No" to Satan and finally sent him away.

Then Jesus began to travel around his homeland, Palestine, telling people about God his Father. He called twelve men to come and follow him. These men, the **apostles,** left their jobs and homes and traveled everywhere with Jesus, learning from him.

People loved to come and hear Jesus tell stories when he visited their towns. Jesus told **parables,** stories that teach about God and his kingdom.

One of Jesus' most famous parables compares God to a man whose son took his money and ran away from home. Most people would be angry and refuse to forgive that son. But the father in Jesus' story forgave his son and welcomed him home (Based on Luke 15:11–32). Jesus used this parable to show how God forgives sinners who return to him (Luke 15).

Jesus also worked many **miracles.** He healed people who were sick or had disabilities. He brought dead people back to life. He calmed the sea when he and his friends were in a boat during a storm.

One of his most famous miracles happened when a large crowd had come to see and hear him. Jesus wanted to give them something to eat, but there were only a few loaves of bread and some fish. Jesus told the apostles to give the food to the crowd and as they did this they found they had enough to feed five thousand people and still have twelve baskets of food left over!

Jesus did all these wonderful things to help people believe that he is God and that he was sent by God the Father.

A Coded Message about Jesus

Below are some statements about Jesus, but the vowels are missing. Do the math problems and find the vowel that matches the answer. Write the correct vowel in each blank.

$$A = 3 \quad E = 5 \quad I = 9 \quad O = 1 \quad U = 7$$

JESUS...

1. w ___ nt t ___ th ___ d___ s ___ rt t ___ pr ___ y.

2	9	10	0	8	19	9
+3	−8	−5	+5	−3	−18	−6

2. h ___ d tw___ lv ___ ___ p ___ stl ___ s.

23	1	6	12	11	15
−20	+4	−1	−9	−10	−10

3. w ___ rk ___ d m ___ r ___ cl ___ s.

3	25	7	12	13
−2	−20	+2	−9	−8

4. ___ s ___ ___ r S ___ v ___ ___ r.

11	16	17	10	6	8
−2	−15	−10	−7	+3	−7

Jesus' Last Days

Catechism paragraphs 571–573, 610–612, 624–627, 629, 638–647, 656, 658, 1194

Just as we remember Jesus' birth and early life during Advent and Christmas time, we remember the last days of his life during Lent and **Easter.**

During **Lent,** we spend forty days saying extra prayers and making sacrifices. We recall that he came to teach us how to live and that he died to free us from our sins.

The last week of Lent is called *Holy Week.* It begins on **Palm Sunday** when we hear the story of Jesus' entry into Jerusalem. A crowd of people welcomed him, waving palm branches and cheering, "Hosanna!"

On **Holy Thursday,** we follow Jesus and his apostles to a special supper they ate for the Jewish feast of Passover. Jesus knew it was his last supper with his friends. During the meal, he blessed bread and wine and said, "This is my Body. This is my Blood. Do this in memory of me."

We call the next day **Good Friday.** After supper on Thursday night, Jesus was arrested. Jesus was taken to the governor, Pontius Pilate, for a trial. Pilate could see Jesus was not guilty, but Jesus' enemies had stirred up the crowd. Now, instead of cheering, "Hosanna," this same crowd shouted, "Crucify him!" Pilate was afraid to let Jesus go free.

They made Jesus carry a heavy beam of wood up a hill called Calvary and hung him on that wooden cross to die. Jesus' mother and some friends took his body and buried it in a tomb. He stayed in the tomb until Sunday morning.

On the first Easter, some women went to the tomb first. They found it empty. An angel came to tell them, "Jesus is not here! He has risen!" This was Jesus' greatest miracle— his resurrection.

When we go to Mass on *Holy Saturday* night, we find the church as dark as a tomb. But we know *Easter Sunday* is about to begin! Jesus did not stay in his tomb and we do not stay in the dark!

Know Our Catholic Tradition

A large Easter Candle reminds us Jesus is the Light of the World.
Flowers, ringing bells, and songs of "Alleluia! Alleluia!"
tell us Jesus has risen and is still with us.

Word Search

Find and circle the answers to the clues below in this letter grid. Be careful! Words can go in all directions.

```
                      R
              T       E       T
          T       O   S   J   F
      K   Q   M   U   V   N       I
  T   O   S   B   R   E   A   D   P
B   J   E   U   B   R   R   D   J   X   U
Y H P E M D E R H Y C A       I
M L O A Q C R V Z A A C       D
C R O S S L T W O T N L       S
J W S T A S I A D I L E       C
B C Q E L N O A G N M N       E
T W Z R E C N V R L R T       H
F Q C C M R P A E M N L
  R N D R U R A Q R C
      I J C U Y I I C K
        A A I G L D
              F C R
              Y G A
                I
                G
```

Clues

1. Word in an Easter song
2. Food that became Jesus' Body at the Last Supper
3. Sign that Jesus is the Light of the World
4. Where Jesus hung until he died
5. What the crowd shouted for Pilate to do to Jesus
6. Feast to celebrate Jesus' rising from the dead.
7. The "Good" day when Jesus died
8. What the crowd shouted as they waved palm branches
9. Forty days to remember Jesus' death for our sins
10. Jewish feast Jesus celebrated at his Last Supper
11. Jesus' greatest miracle—rising from the dead
12. Where Jesus' body was buried
13. Drink that became Jesus' Blood at the Last Supper

Catechism paragraphs 487–495, 508–509

God kept his promise to send a Savior by sending his own Son, Jesus. But God needed a very special person to help him! If he was going to send his Son as a human baby, he would need a mother.

Long before she was born, long before she even began to grow inside her own mother, God chose Mary to be his Son's mother. She is the only person who, from the very beginning of her life, was always without any sin, even original sin. Mary lived her whole life without sinning. She grew up in the town of Nazareth in a Jewish family. She learned to pray and to wait for God to send a Savior.

Even though God had chosen Mary to be his mother, he still needed to find out if she would agree to his plan. God gave Mary free will, just like us, and she had to choose whether to say "Yes" to God or not. So, God sent his messenger, the angel Gabriel, to ask Mary to be the Mother of God. We remember Gabriel's greeting to Mary each time we pray, "Hail, Mary, full of grace, the Lord is with you!"

Mary did not know how she could be God's mother. She was not married. But she knew she could trust God, and she wanted to obey him. Mary said, "I am the servant of the Lord. Let it be done to me as God has said" (Luke 2).

God had chosen the right young woman! Mary became the Mother of God. She named her baby, Jesus. Before Jesus was born, she married Joseph. Now Jesus had a foster father to help take care of him.

When Jesus died on the cross, he asked his apostle John to take care of Mary. "There is your son," he told her. When Jesus did this, he *gave Mary to all of us.* Mary is the Mother of the Church.

Know Our Catholic Belief

Mary, who would one day become the Mother of God, began her own life without any sin at all. This is a great mystery of our faith. We call this mystery the **Immaculate Conception**.

Fill-in Puzzle

The words listed below are about Mary. Find where each word fits on the puzzle grid. The first one has been done for you.

angel	free	Gabriel	hail
immaculate	Jesus	Joseph	miracle
mother	Nazareth	Savior	wine
yes			

Catechism paragraphs 946–948, 954–960

Since Jesus died and rose from the dead, the gates of heaven have been opened. Now, the souls of those who have died after living good and faithful lives go to heaven. In heaven, these souls see and adore God face-to-face.

We call those good and faithful people **saints.** We are all called to be saints! God made each of us to know, love, and serve him while we are on earth and to live with him forever in heaven.

It is not always easy to be good and faithful. We like to hear about people who have gone before us who lived good lives. Their lives can show us how to be saints, too.

Some saints are very well-known. Everyone has heard of the greatest saint of all, Saint Mary, our Blessed Mother! Her husband, Joseph, is also a great saint. What other saints do you know?

Have you heard of Saint Peter? He was one of Jesus' apostles. Jesus chose him to be the first leader of the Church. You can read about him in the New Testament.

Other saints lived long after the Bible was written. There are many books that tell about the lives of the saints. Some saints, like St. Francis Xavier, had great adventures and traveled far to tell people about God. Other saints, like St. Therese of Jesus, hardly traveled at all, but lived each ordinary day in a holy way.

What do all these saints have in common? They lived very different lives, but each one loved, obeyed, and served God by serving others in some way. We can each be saints, too.

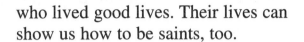

Know Our Catholic Tradition

We Catholics often have the name of a saint. We call the saint whose name we have, our **patron saint.** Do you know who your patron saint is? If you don't, ask someone in your family if they can help you find out about your patron saint.

A Telephone Code Message

To solve this puzzle, use the telephone keypad below. Only one letter from each phone number is needed to solve each blank of the puzzle. Choose the correct letters and you will have a message about our faith.

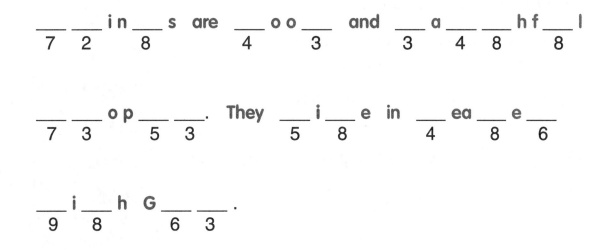

___ ___ i n ___ s are ___ o o ___ and ___ a ___ ___ h f ___ l
7   2   8   4   3   3   4   8   8

___ ___ o p ___ ___ . They ___ i ___ e in ___ ea ___ e ___
7   3   5   3   5   8   4   8   6

___ i ___ h G ___ ___ .
9   8   6   3

Review

Choose from the words that follow to complete the sentences below. Be careful! Not all the words that appear will be used.

1. We can believe what we do not understand about God by using our gift of _____.

2. There are three _____ in one God.

3. The Holy Trinity is a _____ of faith.

4. God created everything out of _____.

5. God created human beings in his own _____.

6. God wants us to choose what we will do by using our free _____.

7. The sin of Adam and Eve is called _____ sin.

8. _____ tempted Adam and Eve.

9. God promised to send a _____.

10. The Christmas Season includes _____ Sundays after Christmas Day.

11. The Resurrection is Jesus' greatest _____.

12. _____ never had original sin on her soul.

13. Saints are in _____ with God.

Eve
faith
four
heaven
home
image
Mary
miracle
mortal
mystery
nothing
original
persons
Satan
Savior
spirits
three
will

Section Two
Our Catholic Celebrations

By now you are familiar with several Catholic celebrations. You celebrate the Mass with your parish community each week and are learning more of the prayers of the Mass. You might even be an altar server!

What sacraments have you celebrated? Have you been baptized? Do you receive the Eucharist when you go to Mass? Are you able to celebrate the sacrament of Reconciliation regularly? Have you received the sacrament of Confirmation yet?

If you have been very ill, you might have received the sacrament of the Anointing of the Sick. What other sacrament do you hope to celebrate some day? Will you become a deacon or a priest by receiving Holy Orders? Will you become a husband or a wife by celebrating Holy Matrimony?

All sacraments are
Signs of God's love,
given to us by Jesus by
which we receive grace.

In this section, you will study each of the seven sacraments to review what you already know and to learn some new facts about how we Catholics celebrate our faith.

Catechism paragraphs 1131, 1262, 1302–1303, 1391, 1468, 1520–1523, 1585, 1641, 2003

All through our lives, God offers us a share in his own life. We call this gift of God's life, **grace.**

God gives us grace as a free gift. He offers it to everyone. But it is up to us to accept God's grace and to use it to help us live good lives.

One special kind of grace is **sacramental grace,** which we receive in the seven **sacraments.** Each sacrament is given to help us live good lives in some way. In each of these signs of God's love, we receive a different sacramental grace to help us in a certain way.

In **Baptism,** Jesus gives us the grace of new life. When we are baptized, we are set free from all sin, especially original sin. We become members of the Body of Christ, the Church.

Through **Confirmation,** the sacramental grace of Baptism is increased and deepened, and we are filled with the gifts of the Holy Spirit.

The grace of the **Eucharist** is the greatest grace of all! We eat the Body of Christ and we drink his Blood. In this holy food, Jesus feeds our souls and makes us strong to live good lives.

In the sacrament of **Reconciliation,** Jesus not only gives us forgiveness of our sins, but gives us grace to turn away from our sins and to live good lives.

In the **Anointing of the Sick,** Jesus may bring healing of body and soul when we are sick. It sometimes helps a sick person become well again. If the person cannot recover, this sacrament brings peace and helps the person to die with faith in God.

In **Holy Orders,** Jesus gives special grace to men chosen to be deacons, priests, or bishops. They receive power to serve God, to care for people, and to lead others to God.

In **Matrimony,** Jesus gives men and women the special grace they will need to live together as husbands and wives. Matrimony helps them to be faithful and to love each other and their children.

Sacramental Grace

Cross out each X and Z in the puzzle. Then cross out the name of each sacrament. Write the remaining letters on the lines below to name the grace of each sacrament.

```
1    X N E B A P T I S M Z W L I X Z F E X X
2    Z C O N F I R M A T I O N S P I R X I T
3    H O L Y F O O X D Z E U C H A R I S T Z
4    X R E C O N C I L I A T I O N N O S I N
5    A N O I N T I N G Z H E A X L I N G Z X
6    Z H O L Y X O R D E R S X S E R V I C E
7    M A X T R I M O N Y Z F A I T H F U L Z
```

1. In Baptism, we receive the grace of ___ ___ ___   ___ ___ ___ ___ .

2. In Confirmation, Jesus gives us the gifts of the

   Holy ___ ___ ___ ___ ___ ___ .

3. In Eucharist, Jesus feeds our souls

   with ___ ___ ___ ___   ___ ___ ___ ___ .

4. After we celebrate Reconciliation, we

   have ___ ___   ___ ___ ___ on our souls.

5. In the Anointing of the Sick, Jesus may bring the

   grace of ___ ___ ___ ___ ___ ___ ___ .

6. In Holy Orders, Jesus blesses men to give

   ___ ___ ___ ___ ___ ___ ___ in the Church.

7. In Matrimony, Jesus gives husbands and wives the

   grace of ___ ___ ___ ___ ___ ___ ___ ___ love.

Sacraments of Initiation

Catechism paragraphs 1213–1216, 1267–1270, 1275, 1277–1278, 1280, 1285, 1293–1296,1316–1317

Baptism and Confirmation are two of our three **sacraments of initiation.** Initiation means "becoming a member." Through Baptism and Confirmation, we become members of the Church.

You know the main sign of Baptism is *water.* A priest or deacon pours the water or places us in the water as he says, "I baptize you in the name of the Father, and of the Son, and of the Holy Spirit." Just as water in nature gives life, so the water of Baptism gives new life to our souls.

Two kinds of *oil* are used at Baptism. One is used to ask God to keep us strong and to protect us from evil. The second blesses us and marks us as God's children.

There are other objects used at Baptism as signs of God's grace. One of these is a *white garment,* a sign of the baptized person's clean, white soul.

Another sign is the *candle.* The large Easter Candle is lit during each Baptism as a sign of the light of Christ. From that candle, a small baptismal candle is lit for the newly baptized person. We are to carry the light of Christ with us after we are baptized.

Initiation into the Church continues with the sacrament of Confirmation. Confirmation completes Baptism, so it shares one of the signs of Baptism. When we are confirmed, a bishop or priest once again blesses us with *oil.* This time the oil is used to *seal us with the Holy Spirit.* The bishop *lays his hand* on us and makes the Sign of the Cross on our foreheads with oil. He says, "Be sealed with the Gift of the Holy Spirit."

In these two sacraments of initiation, God gives us grace so we can be faithful members of the Church. We receive both of these sacraments *only once.* Each one gives our souls a special mark called a **character,** a permanent sign that we are adopted children of God.

We receive the third sacrament of initiation many times. We will read about the sacrament of the Holy Eucharist in the next lesson.

Facts in Code

Use the code to complete the statements about Baptism and Confirmation.

CODE:	A	B
1	water	oil
2	Holy Spirit	Church
3	initiation	members
4	souls	character
5	once	grace

1. Baptism and Confirmation are sacraments of _____

                                                                3A

   because in them God gives us_____ to be faithful

                                              5B

   _____ of the _____.

         3B   2B

2. _____ is used in both Baptism and Confirmation to

       1B

   mark us as God's children, but _____ is only used in

                                            1A

   Baptism as a sign of new life.

3. A priest or deacon says, "I baptize you in the name of the Father,

   and of the Son, and of the _____," as he pours or

                                    2A

   places us in the _____.

                         1A

4. At Confirmation, we receive the gifts of the _____

                                                            2A

   when the bishop makes the Sign of the Cross on our foreheads

   with _____.

         1B

5. We receive Baptism and Confirmation only _____

                                                          5A

   because they mark our _____ with a special mark

                                4A

   called a _____.

               4B

Catechism paragraphs 1322–1324, 1377–1381, 1409–1413

The third sacrament of initiation is the Holy Eucharist. We are welcomed at the table of the Lord. We can eat the Body of Christ and drink his Blood because we are members of the People of God, the Church.

In the Holy Eucharist, Jesus feeds our souls. We receive the grace to be faithful members of the Church.

Jesus gave us the Eucharist the night before he died. He ate his Last Supper with his apostles. While they were eating, Jesus took a piece of bread and blessed it. He broke it and gave some to each person and said, "This is my Body."

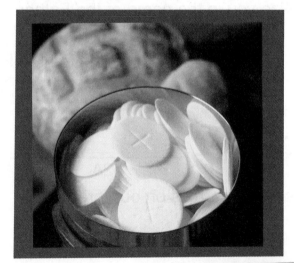

Then Jesus took a cup of wine, blessed it and said, "This is my Blood. Do this in memory of me."

That night, Jesus gave us his Body and Blood as a **holy** meal.

During Jesus' time, people used to kill animals to make a **sacrifice** to God, asking him for special blessings. The day after his Last Supper, Jesus died on the cross. He didn't offer the blood of an animal to God. He gave God his own Body and Blood in a painful sacrifice.

Now the Church does what Jesus told us to do. We gather together to celebrate the **Mass.** The priest consecrates the bread and wine. They become the Body and Blood of Christ when the priest consecrates them. Because of Jesus' actions at his Last Supper, the Mass is a holy meal. Because of Jesus' death on the cross, the Mass is a holy sacrifice. When we receive Holy Communion, we eat the Body of Christ and drink his Blood. We share in the holy meal first given to the apostles at the Last Supper.

Know Our Catholic Tradition

At Mass the priest says, "Pray, my brothers and sisters, that our sacrifice may be acceptable to God the Father Almighty." We answer: "May the Lord accept the sacrifice at your hands for the praise and glory of his name, for our good and the good of all his Church."

A Meal and a Sacrifice

The Mass is both a meal and a sacrifice. When we go to Mass, we can hear words about the Mass as a meal and other words about the Mass as a sacrifice. Below are some parts of prayers from the Mass. Write **meal** next to those that remind you the Mass is a meal. Write **sacrifice** next to those that remind you the Mass is a sacrifice.

"In memory of his death and resurrection, we offer you, Father, this life-giving bread, this saving cup."

_____

_____

"Lord God, Lamb of God, you take away the sin of the world; have mercy on us."

"Through your goodness we have this bread to offer, which earth has given and human hands have made. It will become for us the bread of life."

_____

_____

"Happy are those who are called to his supper."

"Bless and approve our offering; make it acceptable to you, an offering in spirit and in truth."

_____

"Let it become for us the Body and Blood of Jesus Christ, your only Son, our Lord."

_____

"You have gathered us here around the table of your Son."

_____

Holy Orders

Catechism paragraphs 1536, 1554–1571, 1592–1596

While Jesus was with his apostles on earth, he founded his Church. He made Saint Peter the head of the Church. He gave the apostles the power to forgive sins, to teach, to preach, and to heal. At the Last Supper, he gave them the power to change bread and wine into his Body and Blood.

Jesus told the apostles to be like shepherds and lead people to God the Father. He told them to be like servants and take care of peoples' needs.

Now we have a sacrament in which Jesus gives the Church leaders who follow in the footsteps of the apostles. That sacrament is called *Holy Orders*. When a man receives the Sacrament of Holy Orders, we call this his *ordination*. We say he has been *ordained*, or specially chosen, to serve the Church in a special way.

There are three degrees of Holy Orders. The highest degree is the *Order of Bishop*. Each **bishop** is given all the powers given to the apostles.

Each bishop is the leader of a **diocese,** a group of parishes in one area. The bishop is the *chief teacher* of his diocese. He helps the people of his diocese understand what the Church teaches. He makes decisions for the parishes in his diocese. He celebrates the sacrament of Confirmation. When young men are called to be priests in a diocese, it is the bishop who ordains them.

The second degree of Holy Orders is the *priesthood*. When a man is ordained a **priest,** he has the power through Christ to forgive sins. Through the priest, God changes bread and wine into the Body and Blood of Christ. He helps the bishop in the job of teaching by preaching and leading people in a **parish.**

The third degree of Holy Orders is the **diaconate.** When a man is ordained to the diaconate, he is called a **deacon.** Not long after Jesus died, the apostles saw that they needed help doing all the work of the Church. They could not preach and teach and also have time to help the poor and others in need. So they chose men who could be of special service. They called these men deacons.

Today, deacons help bishops and priests in many ways. They assist at Mass. Sometimes they preach. They are able to baptize and to perform the sacrament of Matrimony. They visit the sick, help the poor, and give service in parishes in many ways.

The Three Degrees of Holy Orders

Follow the arrows. At the end of each line, write the letters you passed.

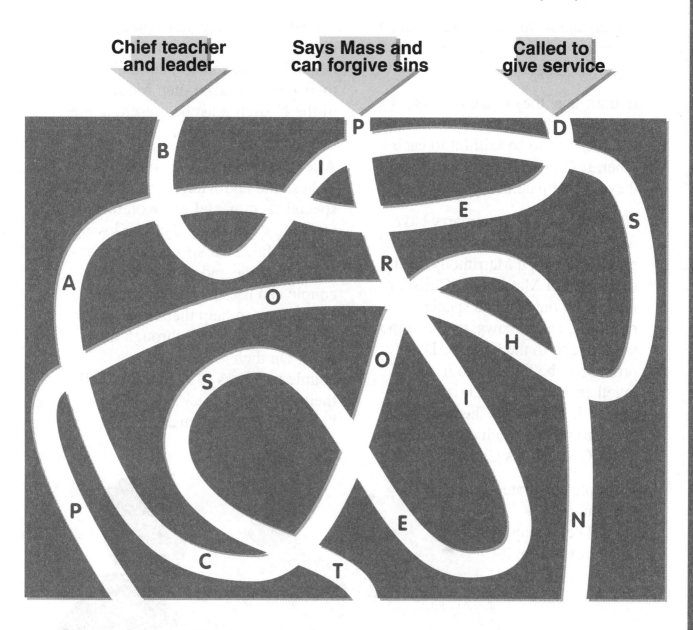

Chief teacher and leader

Says Mass and can forgive sins

Called to give service

_ _ _ _ _ _ _ _   _ _ _ _ _ _   _ _ _ _ _ _ _

Matrimony

Catechism paragraphs 1601, 1630–1631, 1638, 1660, 1662–1663

A man and a woman who love each other and want to share their lives together can get married.

In marriage, they make promises to each other. They promise to live together and to be faithful to each other. If God sends them children, they will be parents.

When the people who marry have faith in Jesus, they receive a special sacrament called Matrimony. In the sacrament of Matrimony, Christian men and women make special promises, called vows, to each other, to God, and to the Church. They promise to be faithful, to live together, and to be a Christian family. If God sends them children, they promise to teach those children about God and his Church.

A couple celebrates Matrimony in a special ceremony called a **wedding.**

Usually a wedding takes place during a Mass. A priest or deacon helps the man and woman make their vows to each other. Members of the Church must be present at the wedding as **witnesses.**

After the wedding, the couple lives as husband and wife. They received special sacramental grace on their wedding day to help them be loving and faithful. That special grace does not stop at the end of that day. The couple can use the special grace of Matrimony to help them every day of their marriage, all through their lives. On their wedding day, a couple promises to stay married all their lives. They make their vows "until death do us part."

Know Our Catholic Tradition

A woman who gets married is called a *bride*. A man who gets married is called a *groom*. Often a bride wears a white wedding dress. Sometimes the bride and groom *exchange rings* at their wedding. They wear wedding rings as a sign that their love will last forever.

Wedding Gifts

People like to get gifts when they get married. In the sacrament of Matrimony, God gives the greatest gifts of all. Fill in each blank, using the clues below and the letters from the word Matrimony already put in place for you.

1. __ __ __ m __ __ __ __

2. __ __ a __ __

3. __ __ __ t __ __ __ __

4. __ __ __ __ r __ __

5. __ i __ __ __

6. __ __ m __

7. __ o __ __ __ __ __ __

8. __ __ __ __ n __

9. __ __ __ __ __ y

1. They make special __ __ __ m __ __ __ __ called vows.

2. Husband and wife receive sacramental __ __ a __ __ to. . .

3. . . . help them be __ __ __ t __ __ __ __.

4. They will be parents if God sends them __ __ __ __ __ r __ __ .

5. Husband and wife want to share their __ i __ __ __ together.

6. They will live in their __ __ m __ .

7. They vow to live __ o __ __ __ __ __ __ forever.

8. They receive grace to be __ __ __ __ n __ and faithful.

9. They promise to live together and to be a Christian __ __ __ __ __ y.

Anointing of the Sick

Catechism paragraphs 1499–1523, 1527–1532

Have you ever been ill? Have you had to stay home in bed with a fever? Were you ever in the hospital? Have you had a broken bone? Have you ever had an operation?

It is never easy to be sick. It makes us sad and scared to feel so bad. Sometimes our illnesses are not serious. We can get well quickly and go back to our usual activities. But even a short or slight illness can be hard.

God knows how hard it is for us to be sick. The Church knows that illness can make a person too weak to pray. Illness can make a person wonder if God loves them. People who are sick need special grace. They need the prayers and blessing of the Church.

Jesus always paid special attention to sick people. When he could, he blessed them and healed them. He also told his apostles to pray for the sick and ask God to heal them.

Before he died, Jesus once said to his followers, "Take up your cross and come follow me" (Matthew 16:24). The Church teaches us that when we are sick, we can share in the sufferings of Jesus. We can carry our crosses as he told us.

Now we have a special sacrament for people who are ill. It is called *the sacrament of the Anointing of the Sick.* A priest places his hands on the sick people and asks God to bless, strengthen, and heal them. Then he anoints them with *oil.*

Sometimes, this sacrament is celebrated during Mass at a parish church. Other times, the priest celebrates the sacrament in the hospital or in the sick person's home. When possible, the sick also receive Holy Communion. The Church wants to give those who are ill all the graces they need to help them heal in mind, body, and soul.

Know Our Catholic Tradition

People who are ill and unable to come to Mass at Church are also included in the prayers of the parish. Often, **Eucharistic ministers** or deacons help the priest by taking Holy Communion to those who are shut-in. Only a priest can give the sacrament of Anointing of the Sick, but we can all pray for the sick.

A Get-well Card

On the closed card, draw or write a design for a religious get-well card.

On the blank inside pages of the card below, write a message and prayer for someone who is ill. Draw pictures inside the card, too, if you like.

Reconciliation

Catechism paragraphs 1422–1426, 1440–1470, 1491, 1494–1495

When you were baptized, all your sins were washed away. But it is not always easy to be good. We sometimes make wrong choices. We choose to hurt someone. Sometimes we lie. Sometimes we disobey. These wrong choices are called *sins*.

We cannot be baptized again, so how can we remove these sins from our souls?

Jesus gave us a wonderful sacrament, the sacrament of Reconciliation.

We can celebrate the sacrament of Reconciliation often. We prepare for it by asking God to help us remember those times when we've sinned, and we tell him how sorry we are.

Sometimes we receive the sacrament in a private celebration.

- We enter the **confessional** or the **reconciliation room** where we sit or kneel and talk to the priest.
- We receive a blessing from the priest. Sometimes he will read a short passage from the Bible.
- We tell him our sins.
- The priest listens and then he talks to us. He gives us advice.

- He also gives us a **penance.** This is a way to show our sorrow for our sins. The penance might be some prayers to say or some action to do after we leave. While we are still with him, the priest asks us to pray a prayer of sorrow, an **Act of Contrition.**
- The priest gives us a blessing, called **absolution,** which forgives all our sins. We are set free from all the things we've done wrong!

We can also receive this sacrament at a **communal Penance service.** We gather at our parish church with others who want to have their sins forgiven. We do not tell our sins to these other people, but we know we are all sinners and we pray for each other. During the Penance service, we

- sing songs,
- listen to Scripture readings and a homily,
- think about our sins,
- and then go and speak privately to a priest and tell him our sins.
- We receive a penance.
- The priest gives us absolution to forgive all our sins.

The sacrament of Reconciliation is Jesus' gift to forgive our sins and make us strong.

Word Search

You can find all the listed words about Reconciliation in the letter grid below. Some words go from left to right. Some go from top to bottom, and some go at a diagonal.

```
            G   J   Z
          D E   W J   E
        B S J   A R G   C
      U Q L   W R   O   O
    S A C R A M E N T   T
    L P Z C E U Y T   G
  P R I E S T S O R R Y
  E A B S O L U T I O N
  N L D S T H Q S T S Y
  A N O B L E S S I N G
  N U J V G O S N O I H
  C O N F E S S N U P
  E C H O I C E S S A R L
    Y F R E E F D A S
    M V G E J V Y P C
    W I Y J I E O J
    C V C R O I J
      E B F T K
      P C B
```

absolution	listens	advice	love
blessing	penance	choices	prayer
confess	priest	contrition	sacrament
forgive	sins	free	sorry
grace	soul	Jesus	wrong

39

Review

Choose words from the following box to complete the sentences below. Be careful! One word will be used twice.

1. Grace is a share in God's _____ which he offers to everyone as a free gift.

2. The sacraments of initiation are _____, _____ and _____.

3. The Mass is both a _____ like Jesus' Last Supper, and a _____ because Jesus died on the cross.

4. The bread and wine become the _____ and _____ of Jesus Christ in the sacrament of the Holy _____.

5. The highest degree of Holy Orders is the Order of _____.

6. In Matrimony, a man and a woman make special promises called _____ to each other.

7. In the sacrament of the Anointing of the Sick, God may give sick people the grace they need to help them _____ in mind, body, and soul.

8. The special blessing through which God forgives our sins in the sacrament of Reconciliation is called _____.

absolution

Baptism

Bishop

Blood

Body

Confirmation

Eucharist

heal

life

meal

sacrifice

vows

We Live Our Life In Christ

We Catholics not only know and celebrate our faith, we also show what we believe by the way we live. We keep God's laws and the laws of the Church. We decide what to do by asking ourselves what Jesus would do. We know the difference between what is right and what is wrong.

As you read these pages and complete these activities, you will review what you know about God's two Great Commandments of Love. You will study each of the Ten Commandments and learn about other ways that we Catholics live our life in Christ as we show our love for God, other people, and ourselves.

Using Your Conscience

Catechism paragraphs 1730–1734, 1745, 1778–1785, 1796, 1798–1804, 1833, 1854–1855, 1871, 1874–1876

One of God's greatest gifts to us is our *free will.* God has given us the power to make choices. We must decide for ourselves whether we will do the right thing or the wrong thing. How can we tell right from wrong?

Sometimes you know the difference deep inside yourself. That inner power to know if something is right or wrong, your *ability to decide* if an action or thing is good or bad, is called your **conscience.** God wants us to listen to our consciences and use our free will to make choices. We must be sure we know enough to make a good choice. That is why we must listen to people who are in charge. We must also read and study about God's laws so we know enough for our consciences to make good choices.

The more good choices you make, the easier it becomes to be good. When doing good becomes a habit, we call that good habit a *virtue.* Virtues are the good things you always or often do. If you always tell the truth, you have the virtue of honesty. If you are generous in helping others, you have the virtue of charity.

Sin is the opposite of virtue. It is *turning away from God's love.* Do you remember the difference between *mortal sin* and *venial sin?*

Mortal sin is so serious that it cuts us off from God's life and love. A sin is mortal when the person knows an action is seriously wrong and freely chooses to do it, which completely turns him or her away from God.

Venial sin is less serious; it does not cut ourselves off from God's life and love. But venial sins are still wrong. They make us weak and make it harder for us to make good choices.

We make decisions about what is right and wrong every day. These kinds of choices are called **moral decisions.**

Think about some of the choices you make. Choosing what color socks to wear or what cereal to eat for breakfast are not moral decisions. But choosing whether to lie or tell the truth is a moral decision. Choosing whether to play nicely or to unfairly fight with a brother or sister is a moral decision. What are some other moral decisions you make? Your conscience will help you make good moral decisions.

Virtue or Sin?

Read about each person below and decide if what they are doing is a **virtue** or a **sin.** Write your choice in the blank after each story.

1. George always gives one-tenth of his allowance in the weekly collection at church.

   _____

2. Mandy threw her apple away at lunch and then told her mom she ate it.

   _____

3. David gave Zack the answers to all the problems on the math test.

   _____

4. Nathan stayed home from Mass last Sunday because he said he was too tired.

   _____

5. When Barbara's mom asks her to play with her little sister, she never complains.

   _____

6. Steve cuts the grass for his grandma every week as a free gift to her.

   _____

7. Jason never lies. You can always believe him.

   _____

8. Juanita took a pack of gum from the store without paying for it.

   _____

9. Judy told the other girls in her class not to talk to or play with Beth.

   _____

10. Jim picks up litter whenever he sees some at the park where he plays.

   _____

The Beatitudes

Catechism paragraphs 1716–1726

Jesus came to tell everyone about the kingdom of God. The people already knew about God's Ten Commandments. Now Jesus wanted them to know more about God's Law of Love. He wanted everyone to know how to be happy. He taught us the **Beatitudes.**

There are eight Beatitudes. We read them in chapter five of Matthew's Gospel.

The first Beatitude is *Blessed are the poor in spirit, for theirs is the kingdom of heaven.* We will be happy if we remember that everything we have comes from God and belongs to God.

The second Beatitude is *Blessed are those who mourn, for they shall be comforted.* We will be happy if we are sorry for our own sins and the sins we see around us.

The third Beatitude is *Blessed are the meek, for they shall inherit the earth.* We will be happy if we do not always try to get our own way or boss other people.

The fourth Beatitude is *Blessed are those who hunger and thirst for justice, for they shall be satisfied.* Jesus knows we will be truly happy if we try hard to give everybody their rights.

The fifth Beatitude tells us *Blessed are the merciful, for they shall obtain mercy.* We can only be happy when we forgive those who have hurt us in some way.

The sixth Beatitude is *Blessed are the pure in heart, for they shall see God.* We will be happy when we use our bodies and minds in the right way as God created us to do.

The seventh Beatitude is *Blessed are the peacemakers, for they shall be called sons of God.* God will call us his children if we make peace with others and love them.

The eighth Beatitude tells us *Blessed are those who are persecuted for goodness' sake, for theirs is the kingdom of heaven.* We must stand up for what is right even if we will be teased or hurt for doing so.

Know Our Catholic Tradition

The Gospel of Matthew tells us that Jesus went up on a mountain to tell his followers about the eight Beatitudes. We often call this sermon described in Matthew, chapter five, *"The Sermon on the Mount."*

Which Beatitude? True or False?

Read each statement below. Write a + in the circle if the statement is true. Write a / if it is false. Then decide which Beatitude the statement is about and write its number on the blank line.

◯ If a bully is picking on your friend, just stay out of the way and keep quiet.

Beatitude # _____

◯ It is good to give an offering of money to thank God for all his gifts to us.

Beatitude # _____

◯ Give everyone a chance to say their opinion if they want to.

Beatitude # _____

◯ You don't have to forgive someone who has hurt you if you don't think they really mean it when they say they are sorry.

Beatitude # _____

◯ It is all right to tell jokes about the private parts of our bodies.

Beatitude # _____

◯ When a drunk driver killed two children, almost everyone in town was sad even if they didn't know the children.

Beatitude # _____

◯ We will be happy if we fight unfairly.

Beatitude # _____

◯ Let a friend choose which game the two of you will play sometimes.

Beatitude # _____

The Works of Mercy

Catechism paragraphs 2443–2448

There are many ways to help others. The Church has listed some of these ways as the *corporal and spiritual works of mercy.* As you read about them, think about which ones you already do. Think about which ones you could try to do. Jesus wants all of us—adults and children—to do these works of mercy to help others.

The **Corporal Works of Mercy** are ways to help in a material way. They are

> Feed the hungry.
> Give drink to the thirsty.
> Clothe the naked.
> Shelter the homeless.
> Visit the sick.
> Visit those in prison.
> Bury the dead.

When you bring a can of soup to a food drive, which work of mercy are you doing? What other corporal works of mercy do you do?

The **Spiritual Works of Mercy** are ways to help in a non-material, or spiritual, way. They are

> Warn the sinner.
> Teach the ignorant.
> Counsel the doubtful.
> Comfort the sorrowing.
> Bear wrongs patiently.
> Forgive all injuries.
> Pray for the living and the dead.

When you listen to a friend who is sad, which work of mercy are you doing? When you help a younger child with her homework, are you doing a work of mercy? What other spiritual works of mercy do you do?

Know Our Catholic Tradition

There are many examples of holy men and women who performed the corporal and spiritual works of mercy in a heroic way. One of these was an American woman named Dorothy Day. Dorothy was born in 1897 and died in 1980. She dedicated her life to helping poor people. She founded the Catholic Worker movement. Today, in many cities, there are still Catholic Worker Houses where men and women can dedicate their lives to helping those who are in great need.

Works of Mercy Headlines

Here are some headlines from newspapers and magazines. Decide which corporal or spiritual work of mercy is being done and write it under the headline.

Red Cross Sets Up Cots for Flood Victims at Local Store

_____

Town Gathers to Pray for Those Who Were Killed

_____

Free Classes in English Each Week at the Library

_____

LOCAL RESTAURANT WILL GIVE FREE THANKSGIVING DINNERS TO THE POOR

_____

Scientist Warns We Must Stop Polluting the Earth

_____

Women's Club Will Provide Gatorade at Rest Stops During MS Walk-A-Thon

_____

Airlines Ships Shoes Free of Charge to Earthquake Victims in Peru

_____

The Laws of the Church

Catechism paragraphs 2041–2043

Let's look at a group of laws that Catholics keep along with the Ten Commandments. Over the years since Jesus ascended into heaven, leaders and members of the Church have seen some laws that everyone needs to know and to keep. These **precepts of the Church** can help our consciences decide what is the right thing to do.

The Precepts of the Church

1. Attend Mass on Sundays and holy days of obligation, and avoid needless work on those days. This law is like the Third Commandment, which tells us to keep Sunday holy. But the Church also wants us to keep other special feast days holy.

2. Receive the sacrament of Reconciliation at least once a year.

3. Receive the sacrament of the Eucharist at least during the Easter season.

4. Observe the days of fasting (for adults this means eating only one meal on certain days) and abstinence (eating no meat).

5. Help provide for the needs of the Church according to your abilities.

Know Our Catholic Tradition

Holy days of obligation:
Feast of Mary, Mother of God—January 1
Feast of the Ascension—forty days after Easter
Feast of the Assumption of Mary into Heaven—August 15
Feast of All Saints—November 1
Feast of Mary's Immaculate Conception—December 8
Feast of the Birthday of Jesus, Christmas—December 25

A Fill-in Puzzle

Use the list of words about the precepts of the Church to fill in the puzzle. One word has already been filled in for you.

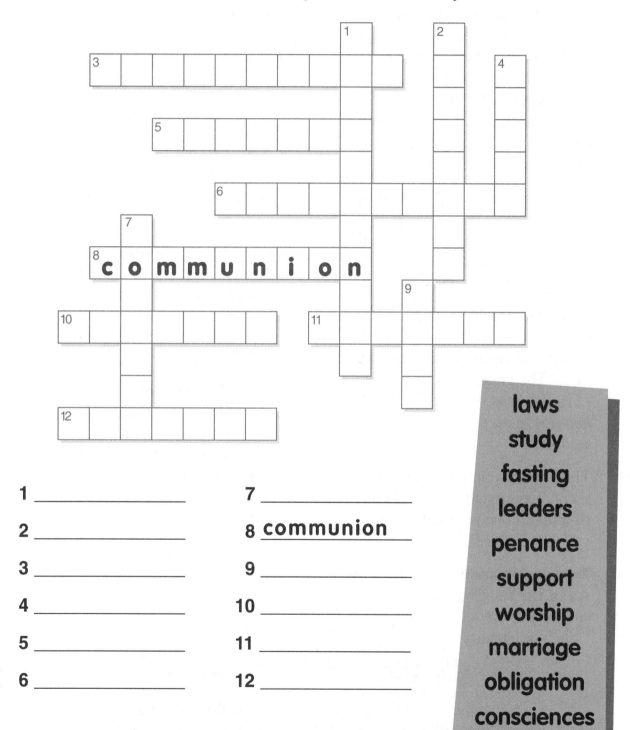

1 _____

2 _____

3 _____

4 _____

5 _____

6 _____

7 _____

8 **communion**

9 _____

10 _____

11 _____

12 _____

laws
study
fasting
leaders
penance
support
worship
marriage
obligation
consciences
missionary

God's Great Laws

Catechism paragraphs 2052–2067

The people of Israel knew about the Ten Commandments for many centuries before Jesus came to teach us about God. Their great leader Moses received the **Ten Commandments** from God while he was leading the people of Israel out of Egypt to their new home in the Promised Land.

Jesus learned the Ten Commandments when he was a boy. He kept the commandments perfectly. One day, to test him, someone asked, "Jesus, which commandment is the greatest?"

Jesus answered that all the Ten Commandments can be summed up in just two Great Commandments. He said, "The greatest commandment is *Love the Lord your God with all your heart, with all your soul, and with all your mind.*"

Then Jesus went on to say, "The second commandment is like the first one: *Love your neighbor as yourself.*" Based on Matthew 22:36-40

Now we can see what Jesus meant. All of the Ten Commandments are summed up in the Two Great Commandments.

The first three commandments tell us how to keep the first Great Commandment, to love the Lord our God. They are

1. I am the Lord your God: You shall not have strange gods before me.
2. You shall not take the name of the Lord your God in vain.
3. Remember to keep holy the Lord's Day.

The last seven commandments tell us how to keep the second Great Commandment, to love our neighbors as ourselves. They say

4. Honor your father and your mother.
5. You shall not kill.
6. You shall not commit adultery.
7. You shall not steal.
8. You shall not bear false witness against your neighbor.
9. You shall not covet your neighbor's wife.
10. You shall not covet anything that belongs to your neighbor.

Know Our Catholic Belief

We read in the Book of Exodus in the Old Testament, "When God finished speaking with Moses on Mount Sinai, he gave him the two tablets of the covenant, tablets of stone, written with the finger of God." Exodus 31:18

A Commandment Mix-up

Sarah's class is making posters about the Ten Commandments. As Sarah was carrying the letters to spell each commandment, she dropped some of them! Can you help her unscramble the letters and put them in the correct order?

You shall not kate the mean of the droL uroy God in naiv.

_____

_____

breemmeR to peek holy the droL's yDa.

_____

_____

I am the Lord your God; You shall not have grenast sodg ebrofe me.

_____

_____

noorH your thearf and your theorm.

_____

_____

You shall not covet uyor neighbor's fewi.

_____

_____

You shall not micmot truelday.

_____

ouY shall not least.

_____

oYu shall not lilk.

_____

You shall not tocev aynngiht that slogben to your bignoreh.

_____

_____

You halls ton rabe slafe stwines against your neighbor.

_____

_____

Honoring God

Catechism paragraphs 2084–2086, 2134–2135, 2142–2155, 2161–2163

The First Commandment might be a surprise to some people. It says *I am the Lord your God: You shall not have strange gods before me.*

What "strange" gods could we have? If we know that God is the one true God, how could we have other "strange" gods? The First Commandment tells us to *put God first.* Even though we believe there is only one God, we can break this commandment by putting other people or other things first.

Sometimes we pay more attention to what people tell us than we do to what God teaches us through his Church. We should listen to others, but we don't put them before God. Sometimes people put money or a car or a job first in their lives. It is good to have those things, but we must not put them first. God comes first.

We keep the First Commandment when we believe in God and put our trust in him. We don't need to worry because we know God will take care of us. God is all-good and all-powerful. There is no one more powerful than God.

The Second Commandment also tells us how to love God. It says *You shall not take the name of the Lord your God in vain.*

God is so good and so holy that we take care to give honor to his name. We speak about God with respect and love. We do not use God's name to swear or to speak in anger. When we speak God's name, we are praying to him and praising him.

God's name is holy, and the many words we use to talk about the Father, Son, and Holy Spirit are special. We must not use these words to be funny or angry or mean.

Know Our Catholic Tradition

We pray "The Divine Praises" as a way to honor God's name. These are some Divine Praises: Blessed be God. Blessed be his holy name. Blessed be Jesus Christ, true God and true man. Blessed be the name of Jesus.

Clues and Transfers

Fill in each blank below to complete each statement. When a line has a number beneath it, transfer that letter to the blank marked with that number at the bottom of the page. When you are finished, the transfers will tell something the First and Second Commandments both teach us to do.

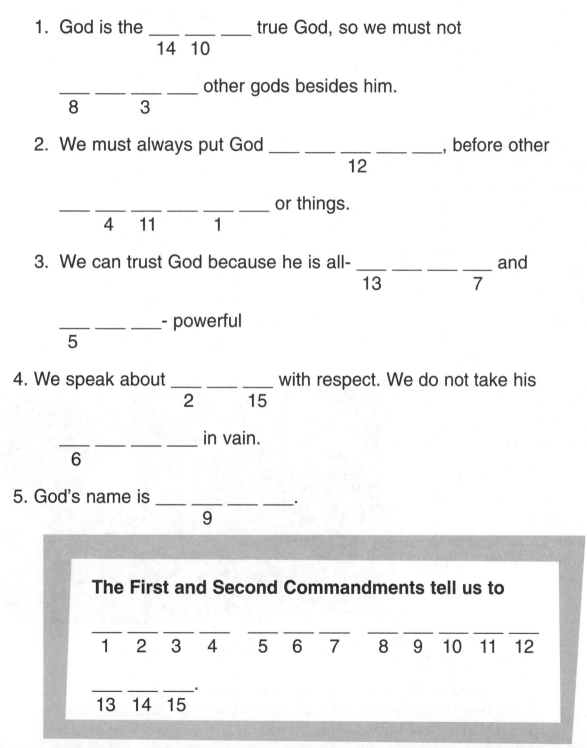

1. God is the ___ ___ ___ true God, so we must not
                   14 10

   ___ ___ ___ ___ other gods besides him.
    8   3

2. We must always put God ___ ___ ___ ___ ___, before other
                        12

   ___ ___ ___ ___ ___ ___ or things.
      4   11   1

3. We can trust God because he is all- ___ ___ ___ ___ and
                             13   7

   ___ ___ ___- powerful
    5

4. We speak about ___ ___ ___ with respect. We do not take his
               2   15

   ___ ___ ___ ___ in vain.
    6

5. God's name is ___ ___ ___ ___.
             9

The First and Second Commandments tell us to

___ ___ ___ ___   ___ ___ ___   ___ ___ ___ ___ ___
1   2   3   4   5   6   7   8   9   10   11   12

___ ___ ___.
13   14   15

Catechism paragraphs 2168, 2174–2185, 2190–2194

The Third Commandment is *Remember to keep holy the Lord's Day*.

Which day is the Lord's Day, and how do we keep it holy? Another name for the Lord's Day is the **Sabbath.**

We read in the Book of Genesis in the Old Testament that, after God worked for six days creating the world, he rested on the seventh day. God told his people he wanted them to do the same. They were to set aside the seventh day as a day for worship and for rest. So, at first, the Lord's Day was Saturday, the seventh day of the week. Then, on a Sunday morning, Jesus rose from the dead. Now, Christians everywhere call **Sunday** the Lord's Day.

We honor God and keep his day holy by going to Mass. We must go to Mass each Sunday or the Saturday evening before it. We Catholics gather together in our churches on Sundays as a sign of our faith in God. We come together with other believers to worship the one true God. This is another way for us to put God first.

Because God rested from the work of creation on the seventh day, we now also try to avoid doing hard work on Sundays. It is a day for resting and having fun! Of course, some jobs have to be done, even on Sunday. Not everyone can take the day off! But we Catholics are called to set Sunday aside as a special day of rest in any way we can. How does your family spend Sundays?

Know Our Catholic Belief

In the Book of Genesis in the Old Testament, we read, "So God blessed the seventh day and hallowed it, because on it God rested from all the work that he had done in creation." Genesis 2:3

A Sunday Newspaper

Use the newspaper pages below to write about how you and your family and friends spend Sundays. Include something about how your family honors God on Sunday. Also tell about how you make Sunday a day of rest. Write something about food you like to eat at a special Sunday meal.

FAMILY NEWS

MY SUNDAY

We Obey

Catechism paragraphs 2197–2200, 2248, 2251, 2255

The Fourth Commandment is *Honor your father and your mother.*

Some people think this commandment is only for children. They think they do not have to obey anyone after they grow up and move away from home. It is true that children must obey their parents, but the Fourth Commandment says much more than this. This commandment is for everyone!

When Jesus lived on earth, he kept the Fourth Commandment, too. Jesus obeyed his parents, Mary and Joseph. But Jesus also obeyed other people who had authority over him. Jesus kept the laws of the land where he lived. He showed respect for people in authority.

Even after you move away from your parents' home, you will keep the Fourth Commandment. You will love your parents and show them respect. If they need help, you will take care of them.

Of course, there are other people we must obey, too. When we obey teachers and other school leaders, coaches, Scout leaders, even babysitters, we are keeping the Fourth Commandment.

We must all obey the laws of our state and country, too. We show respect and we obey police and fire fighters when they are doing their duties for our communities. We are also keeping the Fourth Commandment when we obey traffic signs while walking or riding our bikes.

God wants us to remember that all authority comes from him. People who are in charge must remember that God has given them the job of being leaders. Leaders must never do anything to hurt the people they are leading. Being a good parent or a good leader is part of keeping the Fourth Commandment, too.

Know Our Catholic Belief

St. Paul wrote about the Fourth Commandment in his letter to the Colossians. He wrote, "Children, obey your parents in everything, for this is your acceptable duty in the Lord. Fathers, do not provoke your children, or they may lose heart." Colossians 3:20-21

Authority Wheel Code

Use the authority wheel to complete the following statements.

1. _____ must _____ their _____ .
          L   D   F

2. The Fourth Commandment is not just for _____ .
                                                L

   It is for _____ .
               B

3. _____ had to _____ the _____ of the land.
          A   D   J

4. We must always _____ our _____ and show them
                       C   F

   _____ .
       H

5. We keep the Fourth Commandment when we _____
                                                   H

   and _____ our _____ and other _____ .
          D   E   I

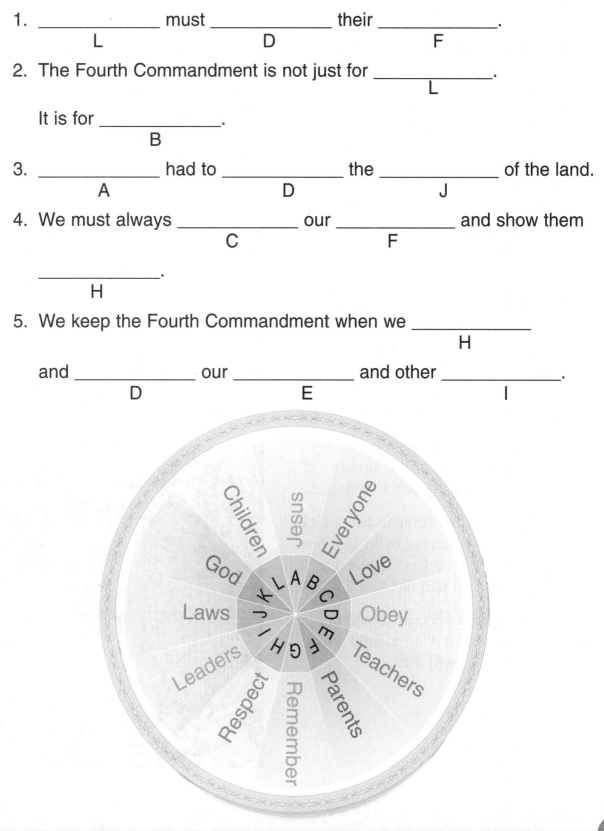

Respect All Life

Catechism paragraphs 2258, 2261, 2288–2291, 2320, 2322–2325

The Fifth Commandment is *You shall not kill.*

This is another commandment that means much more than you might think! You know what a serious crime murder is. Murdering someone is a mortal sin. But not many of us would ever kill another person. How do we keep or break the Fifth Commandment?

God has given each of us the *gift of life.* We keep the Fifth Commandment by protecting and respecting all of life. We must never do anything to harm someone's life or to take someone's life. Only God should decide when someone is to die.

We may not decide that a baby will not be born. It is up to God whether a baby will live or die.

We may not decide to end a sick person's suffering by killing him or her. It is up to God when a sick person will die.

We may not decide to end our own lives. It is up to God when each of us will die.

There are other important ways to show we respect life. We keep the Fifth Commandment when we treat other people with care and respect. We must never do anything to harm anyone, unless it is to protect ourselves or others.

The Fifth Commandment also tells us to take care of our own lives. We must take care of our bodies—eat good foods, wear warm clothes, get enough sleep at night. We must not harm our bodies by using drugs or alcohol or by smoking.

We keep the Fifth Commandment when we care for all life—our own and others'.

A Message in Code

The Book of Deuteronomy in the Old Testament has an important message about the Fifth Commandment. Find out what it is by adding or subtracting letters from the alphabet as directed.
Write the correct letter on the lines.

A B C D E F G H I J K L M
N O P Q R S T U V W X Y Z

$\overline{\text{J-1}}$ $\overline{\text{J-2}}$ $\overline{\text{F-5}}$ $\overline{\text{T+2}}$ $\overline{\text{B+3}}$ $\overline{\text{N+5}}$ $\overline{\text{F-1}}$ $\overline{\text{Q+3}}$ $\overline{\text{A+1}}$ $\overline{\text{H-3}}$ $\overline{\text{J-4}}$ $\overline{\text{L+3}}$ $\overline{\text{V-4}}$ $\overline{\text{D+1}}$

$\overline{\text{W+2}}$ $\overline{\text{P-1}}$ $\overline{\text{W-2}}$ $\overline{\text{P-4}}$ $\overline{\text{K-2}}$ $\overline{\text{E+1}}$ $\overline{\text{C+2}}$ $\overline{\text{C-2}}$ $\overline{\text{L+2}}$ $\overline{\text{A+3}}$

$\overline{\text{G-3}}$ $\overline{\text{G-2}}$ $\overline{\text{G-6}}$ $\overline{\text{P+4}}$ $\overline{\text{K-3}}$ . . . . $\overline{\text{H-5}}$ $\overline{\text{C+5}}$ $\overline{\text{M+2}}$ $\overline{\text{Q-2}}$ $\overline{\text{O+4}}$ $\overline{\text{B+3}}$

$\overline{\text{J+2}}$ $\overline{\text{F+3}}$ $\overline{\text{O-9}}$ $\overline{\text{Q-12}}$!

Based on Deuteronomy 30:19

Our Bodies Are Special

Catechism paragraphs 2331–2336, 2393–2394, 2397, 2521–2522, 2533

Two of the Ten Commandments tell us how we should think about our own and other peoples' bodies. They are the Sixth and the Ninth commandments. We will learn about the two of them together here.

The Sixth Commandment says *You shall not commit adultery.* At first, you might think this is a commandment only for grownups. The word **adultery** means that a married person has not been faithful to the vows of marriage. When married people break their marriage vows, they break the Sixth Commandment.

In the same way, the Ninth Commandment seems to be only for grownups. It says *You shall not covet your neighbor's wife.* To **covet** means to want something that belongs to another so badly that you would do anything to get it. People break the Ninth Commandment when they want to love and marry someone who is already married to someone else.

But what do these two commandments have to do with children? In the Book of Genesis in the Old Testament, we read:

> God created man in his own image…male and female he created them. Genesis 1:27

God gave each of us a body. Some of us are female. Some of us are male. Each of us, male and female, is very special. God created us *in his own image!*

The Sixth and Ninth Commandments remind us we are created in God's image. The male and female parts of our bodies are very private. No one should touch us in a wrong way. We should never touch or look at other people's bodies in a wrong way, even in pictures or movies. We keep the Sixth and Ninth Commandments when we respect each person, male and female.

Know Our Catholic Belief

Here is what St. Paul wrote about our bodies in his first letter to the Corinthians: "Do you not know that your body is a temple of the Holy Spirit within you, which you have from God, and that you are not your own? For you were bought with a price; therefore glorify God in your body." 1 Corinthians 6:19-20

Word Search

You can find the words missing from the sentences below hidden in the letter grid. Watch out! Some words read from side to side, but others read from top to bottom and others from corner to corner.

```
W  D  I  G  M  J  N  Y  T
W  I  F  E  G  R  R  A  O
F  E  M  A  L  E  H  S  U
B  C  X  A  T  S  B  W  C
B  D  O  L  G  P  O  U  H
G  W  U  V  B  E  D  Z  H
R  D  S  P  E  C  I  A  L
A  G  L  J  R  T  E  U  U
T  E  F  V  O  W  S  N  Z
```

Clues

1. The Sixth Commandment says You shall not commit _____.
2. Some parts of our _____ are very private.
3. When we want something that does not belong to us we _____.
4. Some of us are male, and some of us are _____.
5. God created us in his own _____.
6. We keep the Sixth and Ninth Commandments when we _____ each person.
7. Each of us, male and female, is very _____.
8. We must never let someone _____ us in a wrong way.
9. Married people must be faithful to their marriage _____.
10. The Ninth Commandment says You shall not covet your neighbor's _____.

Owning Property

Catechism paragraphs 2401–2408, 2453–2454, 2534–2540, 2552–2553

Here are two more commandments that we can study together. Both of them tell us how to treat other people's property. *Property* means the things a person owns. What are some things that are your property?

The seventh commandment says *You shall not steal.* That seems easy to understand, doesn't it? You already know it is wrong to steal. You know it is wrong to take things that don't belong to you.

But there is more to the Seventh Commandment than this! This commandment also tells us how to treat other people's property. We must take care of things we use which belong to others. We must be respectful and careful of public property. We must never damage anything belonging to another person.

If we borrow anything, we must give it back. We also must take good care of our own property. What do we have that we could own without God's help? All that we have comes from God. We must not even damage our own property.

The Tenth Commandment tells us *You shall not covet your neighbor's goods.* You already know what the word covet means. If you covet your neighbor's goods, that means you want something that belongs to someone else so badly that you would do anything, even hurt your friend, to get it. It also means you wish they did *not* have it!

When you feel bad because someone has something you want, and when you wish they did not have it, you are breaking the Tenth Commandment.

Which Commandment? Keeping or Breaking?

Read each scene below. Then decide which commandment is needed and whether you would be keeping or breaking that commandment if you did the action in the scene. Circle the correct word and fill in the number of the commandment involved.

1. You are very sad that Andy has a new yo-yo just like the one you wanted.

    You are keeping/breaking the _____ *Commandment.*

2. You borrowed a friend's bike. When you returned it, it was in good shape. You even put more air in the tires!

    You are keeping/breaking the _____ *Commandment.*

3. When the person at the check-out counter gave you too much change, you went back to the store to return the money as soon as you saw the mistake.

    You are keeping/breaking the _____ *Commandment.*

4. At your brother's birthday party, you were really happy for him. He got some very nice presents.

    You are keeping/breaking the _____ *Commandment.*

5. You looked over on a classmate's paper and copied some answers during the math test today.

    You are keeping/breaking the _____ *Commandment.*

6. After you had your picnic, your Scout troop picked up your trash, wiped off the picnic tables, put out the campfire, and left the park in good order.

    You are keeping/breaking the _____ *Commandment.*

Telling the Truth

Catechism paragraphs 2464–2470, 2475–2492, 2505, 2507–2508

The Eighth Commandment is *You shall not bear false witness against your neighbor.* This commandment is all about telling the truth.

It is wrong to lie. It is especially wrong to lie about another person. The Eighth Commandment tells us never to speak a lie, especially about another person.

It is very important to Jesus that his followers tell the truth. "I am the way, the truth, and the life," Jesus said (John 14:6). He wanted his apostles to always speak the truth about him. He always spoke the truth about himself and other people.

We must never say anything that will give someone a bad name or a bad reputation. The Eighth Commandment also tells us not to say something mean or bad about a person, even if it is true. Sometimes, we should not say anything at all! It is very hard to take back our words after we have said them. If we speak unkindly or dishonestly about someone, others might repeat what we have said.

It is also wrong to say good things about a person if they are not true. And, of course, it is wrong to brag or to say things that aren't true about ourselves! We keep the Eighth Commandment when we speak the truth about ourselves and others. We also should speak the truth about God and all the good things God has done for us and given us.

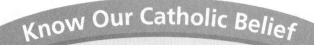

Know Our Catholic Belief

The Book of Sirach in the Old Testament is a book of advice written by a very wise man. Here is what he says about the truth: "Most important of all, pray to God to set your feet in the path of truth." Sirach 37:15

Crossword Puzzle

Solve the puzzle.

Across

2. It is hard to take these back.
3. Jesus always spoke the truth about _____ and other people.
4. We also keep the Eighth Commandment when we speak the truth about the _____ things God has done for us.
6. Sometimes, we should not say _____ at all.
7. We must not bear false _____ against our neighbor.
9. It is especially wrong to lie about another _____.
10. The Eighth Commandment is all about telling the _____.

Down

1. We must never say something that would give a person a bad name or _____.
2. It is _____ to say good things about someone if they are not true.
4. Even if it is true, we should not say something _____ about a person.
8. Who said, "I am the way, the truth, and the life?"

Review

Choose words from the box to complete the sentences below.

1. Your _____ is your ability to _____ if an action or thing is good or bad.

2. God gave you the gift of _____ will so you can make _____.

3. Sin is turning _____ from God's love.

4. _____ sin is very serious. _____ sin is less serious, but still wrong.

5. The Beatitudes teach us how to be _____.

6. The corporal works of mercy help people in a _____ way.

7. Besides the Ten Commandments, Catholics must obey the precepts of the _____.

8. We respect all _____ because we know only _____ can decide when someone will die.

9. God made us male and female and in his own _____.

10. When we _____, it means we want someone or something that does not belong to us.

11. The Seventh and Tenth Commandments tell us how to treat other people's _____.

away
choices
Church
conscience
covet
decide
free
God
image
material
mortal
property
venial
life
happy

Section Four
We Catholics Pray

You have known how to pray for a long time now. You know that prayer is the way we talk to God. Here is a good definition of prayer from the *Catechism of the Catholic Church*. It is a definition written by St. John Damascene.

> **Prayer** is the raising of one's mind and heart to God or the requesting of good things from God.
>
> Catechism paragraph 2559

What are some of your favorite prayers? What are some of your favorite ways to pray?

In this section, you will learn about several forms of prayer and things that Catholics use to help them pray.

You will learn what Jesus taught his apostles when they asked, "Lord, teach us to pray."

Prayer in the Bible

Catechism paragraph 2568–2589

Jesus was born into a Jewish family. His mother, Mary, and his foster father, Joseph, taught him Jewish prayers. The Holy Family prayed together.

The Jewish prayers came from the Old Testament. When Abraham prayed, God revealed himself as the one true God. Abraham and Sarah prayed to God. They taught their children to pray, too.

They prayed to God to ask for his help. They prayed to God to give him praise and to thank him for all he gave them. Because they had great faith in God, they believed he would answer their prayers.

The great Jewish leader Moses prayed to God and became very close to God. Moses talked to God face-to-face.

Some of the most famous prayers in the Old Testament were written by the great King David. David was one of Jesus' ancestors. He was a great king and warrior, but he was also a poet and a musician. So David wrote prayers the people could sing. We call these prayers **psalms.**

We find the psalms of David and of other songwriters in the Book of Psalms in the Old Testament.

The Jewish people prayed the psalms whenever they gathered to worship God. Jesus prayed the psalms all through his life. Even when he was dying on the cross, he prayed words from one of the psalms:

> My God, my God, why have you abandoned me?
>
> Psalm 22:1

Now, we Catholics pray the psalms. When we use the psalms to pray, we praise and thank God and ask him to bless us and other people. At Mass, during the **Liturgy of the Word,** we sing or pray the *Responsorial Psalm.*

Know Our Catholic Tradition

When we pray or sing a Responsorial Psalm, the lector leads us by proclaiming a line of the psalm called the antiphon. We repeat an antiphon like this one after the lector reads each verse of the psalm:

Antiphon: Make a joyful noise to the Lord, all the earth. Worship the Lord with gladness; come into his presence with singing.

From Psalm 100

Who Am I?

The clues below will tell you about some people who prayed in the Bible. Write the correct name for each person described below.

I was a king, but also a poet. The prayers I wrote are still prayed and sung by people today.

Who am I? _____

I talked to God face-to-face.

Who am I? _____

We pray the psalms at Mass today, especially during the Liturgy of the Word.

Who are we? _____

I prayed a psalm while I was dying.

Who am I? _____

My wife and I raised our son in a Jewish family. We taught him how to pray the prayers of the Old Testament.

Who are we? _____

We taught our children to pray to the one true God.

Who are we? _____

We are a people who prayed the psalms whenever we gathered to worship God. Jesus was one of us and prayed with us.

Who are we?

The _____ **people**

Catholics Pray Together

Catechism paragraphs 1163–1178, 1187, 2720

When we Catholics pray together, we call the prayer **liturgy** or *liturgical prayer.* Liturgy is the public worship of God.

Each time we go to Mass, we celebrate the **Liturgy of the Eucharist.** This is the group of prayers we pray together as the priest blesses bread and wine and they become the Body and Blood of Christ.

Each celebration of a sacrament also has its own special prayers, its own liturgy.

No matter what Catholic church you go to, the prayers of the liturgy are the same. Each parish has a special book called the **Sacramentary** that contains the prayers for each liturgy. Each Sacramentary contains the same prayers. You will feel at home in any Catholic church when you go there to celebrate a liturgy!

God has given us the gift of our time. So the Church marks each hour of the day and each day of the year as holy. This helps us remember that all of our times comes from God and belongs to God.

You have already learned some things about the **liturgical year.** It is the year marked off in holy seasons: *Advent, Christmas, Lent,* and *Easter.*

The first day of the liturgical year is the *first Sunday of Advent.* Look on a calendar and see when the new liturgical year will begin this year. In which part of the calendar will you look? (Hint: For what feast day does Advent prepare us? Where is that day found on the calendar? How many Sundays before that are Sundays of Advent? You can review this in Section One.) The first Sunday of Advent is a sort of New Year's Day.

The Church all over the world begins the liturgical year on the first Sunday of Advent.

The prayers and actions of each liturgy, the liturgical seasons, and the books that guide the liturgy, help all of us pray together in public. This liturgical prayer is an important part of being a Catholic.

Know Our Catholic Tradition

When Catholics gather to pray, we often sing some of our prayers. Sometimes we sing psalms, and sometimes we sing other spiritual songs called hymns. Many hymns have been written especially for certain seasons of the liturgical year.

A Fill-in Puzzle

Fill the words about liturgy into the puzzle below. One word has been filled in for you. After you fill in all the words, copy the letters that are in the circles. Unscramble them and they will tell you the kind of worship the liturgy is.

Liturgy is ___ ___ ___ ___ ___ ___ worship.

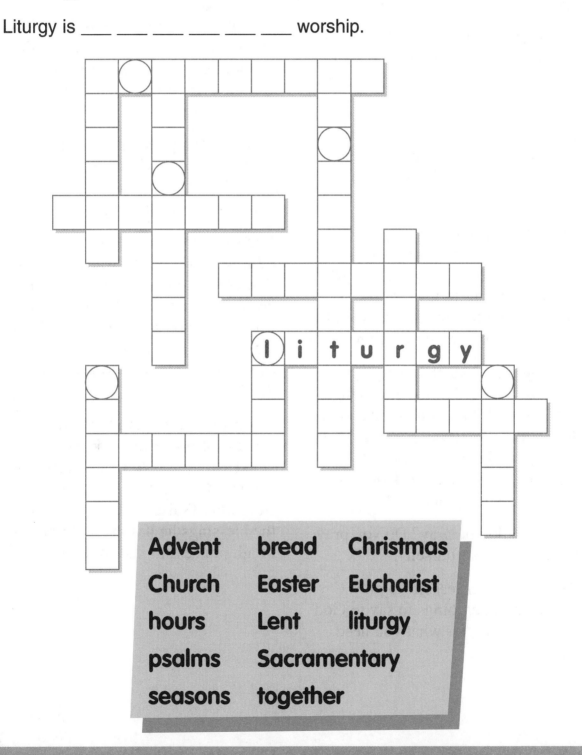

Advent   bread   Christmas

Church   Easter   Eucharist

hours   Lent   liturgy

psalms   Sacramentary

seasons   together

Praying Alone

Catechism paragraphs 2626–2644, 2697–2708, 2721

We often pray with other people. It is also good to talk to God when we are alone.

You can pray the Lord's Prayer or the Hail Mary or any other prayer you have memorized. You can also learn new prayers.

At other times, you might want to pray in your own words. You can talk to God at any time and say anything you want to say.

Sometimes you might pray by thinking of a story about Jesus or Mary and talking to God about what the story means to you or how you want to be more like Jesus. We call this kind of prayer **meditation.**

Often when we think of prayer, we think of asking God for something. Jesus himself told us to ask his Father for anything we need. He said, "Ask and you will receive; seek and you will find; knock and the door will be opened to you" (Luke 11:9).

For what do you pray? Do you pray for others? For yourself?

There are other reasons to pray. There are other things to say to God besides asking for what you need.

You can pray prayers of **adoration** to God. You **adore** God when you tell him you know he is all-powerful, all-good, and all-holy. You know you are only a creature made by God. Prayers of adoration tell God how great he is and how much you need him.

You can also pray a prayer of *contrition* to tell God you are *sorry* and ask him to forgive you when you've done something wrong.

You should always remember to say *"Thank you"* to God when you pray. Remember to thank God whenever he answers a prayer. Thank God for everything you have and all that you are and can do. God gives us everything. It is right to give him thanks!

It is also right to give God *praise.* Prayers of praise tell God how wonderful he is. You know he is the one true God and all blessings come from him. Praise God not only for the blessings he has given, but most of all, praise him just for being God.

Which Kind of Prayer?

Decide if each prayer below is a prayer of—

asking

adoration

contrition

thanks

praise

Write the correct choice after each prayer.

1. "O my God, I am sorry that I have sinned."

   This is a prayer of _____.

2. "Give us this day our daily bread."

   This is a prayer of _____.

3. "Forgive us our trespasses, as we forgive those who trespass against us."

   This is a prayer of _____.

4. "Holy, holy, holy Lord, God of power and might!"

   This is a prayer of _____.

5. "God, you are so wonderful!"

   This is a prayer of _____.

6. "Jesus, I am so grateful for all you have done for me."

   This is a prayer of _____.

7. "Holy Spirit, please help me with my schoolwork today."

   This is a prayer of _____.

Praying to Jesus

Catechism paragraphs 2665–2669

When we are praying alone or when we are praying with others, we can pray a special form of meditation called the Way of the Cross.

The next time you go to your parish church, look along the walls. There are probably some statues or pictures placed a few feet apart all around the church that tell the story of how Jesus died on the cross. We call these statues or pictures the Stations of the Cross. Each one shows a different scene that took place on Good Friday when Jesus died.

We can pray the Way of the Cross by walking around the church and stopping near each Station to think about what Jesus did to save us from our sins. We can pray to him and thank him for dying on the cross for us. We ask him to forgive our sins.

There are fourteen Stations of the Cross. Some of them come from the stories of Jesus' crucifixion in the Gospels. Others come from Church tradition. Try to pray the Way of the Cross by thinking about each Station as you read them now.

The first Station: Jesus is condemned to death.

The second Station: Jesus accepts his cross.

The third Station: Jesus falls the first time.

The fourth Station: Jesus meets his mother.

The fifth Station: Simon helps Jesus carry his cross.

The sixth Station: Veronica wipes Jesus' face.

The seventh Station: Jesus falls the second time.

The eighth Station: Jesus meets some weeping women.

The ninth Station: Jesus falls again.

The tenth Station: Jesus is stripped of his clothes.

The eleventh Station: Jesus is nailed to the cross.

The twelfth Station: Jesus dies.

The thirteenth Station: Jesus' body is taken down from the cross and given to his mother.

The fourteenth Station: Jesus is buried in a tomb.

Know Our Catholic Tradition

When we pray the Stations of the Cross, we pray at each station, "We adore you, O Christ, and we praise you, because by your holy Cross you have redeemed the world."

Drawing Some Stations of the Cross

Choose six of the fourteen Stations of the Cross and draw a picture of each one in one of the boxes below. At the bottom of the page, write a prayer to Jesus, in your own words, about his dying on the cross for you.

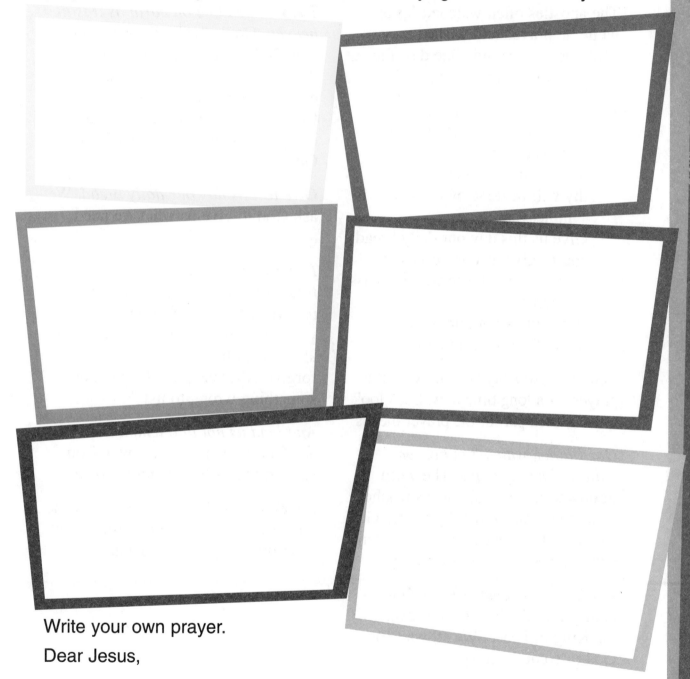

Write your own prayer.

Dear Jesus,

_____

_____

_____

The Lord's Prayer

Catechism paragraphs 2761–2865

The apostles often watched Jesus while he prayed and wished they could pray as he did. One day, they asked, "Lord, teach us to pray."

Jesus said, "When you pray, say,
Our Father, who art in heaven,
hallowed be thy name;
thy kingdom come;
thy will be done on earth as it is in heaven.
Give us this day our daily bread;
and forgive us our trespasses
as we forgive those who trespass against us;
and lead us not into temptation,
but deliver us from evil."

You have probably been praying this prayer for a long time now. Let's look at what each part of the prayer means.

Our Father, who art in heaven, hallowed be thy name. The word **hallowed** means holy. Jesus teaches us to begin our prayer by telling God we know he is our Father in heaven and that we know he is all-holy.

Thy kingdom come. We ask God to come and rule the world forever as the King of Peace. We all wait for God to come in glory.

Thy will be done on earth as it is in heaven. God's "will" is everything that God wants. In heaven, everyone does what God wants, but here on earth, people choose to turn away from God. We pray that, one day, everyone on earth will also do what God wants.

Give us this day our daily bread. We ask God to give us what we need today.

Forgive us our trespasses, as we forgive those who trespass against us. We ask God to forgive the things we have done wrong, but only if we also accept the grace of God to also forgive other people who have done something wrong to us!

And lead us not into temptation. We ask God to help us stay away from sin and things that tempt us to sin.

But deliver us from evil. We know the whole world needs God to protect us from the evil power of Satan.

Matching Meanings

Match the parts of the Lord's Prayer on the left with their meanings on the right. Do this by labeling the part of the prayer with the letter in front of its meaning. Place letters in the boxes provided.

1. Our Father, who art in heaven, hallowed be thy name.

2. Thy kingdom come.

3. Thy will be done on earth as it is in heaven.

4. Give us this day our daily bread.

5. And forgive us our trespasses, as we forgive those who trespass against us.

6. And lead us not into temptation.

7. But deliver us from evil.

a. We ask for what we need.

b. We wait for God to come in glory and rule us forever.

c. We want to stay away from sin.

d. God our Father is all-holy.

e. We want to do whatever God wants.

f. We are sorry for the things we have done wrong, and we know we also must forgive anyone who has hurt us.

g. The whole world needs protection from the power of Satan.

Section Four
Review

Choose words from the box to complete the sentences below. Be careful! Not all the words on the list will be used and one will be used twice.

1. Liturgy is the _____ worship of God.

2. You will feel at _____ in any Catholic church because they all use the same _____ from the Sacramentary.

3. The Church's liturgical _____ marks off special seasons.

4. The first Sunday of _____ is a sort of "New Year's Day" for the Church.

5. _____ is prayer we say by thinking about a story of Jesus or Mary and talking to God about what it means to us.

6. Prayers of _____ tell God how wonderful he is.

7. The Way of the _____ is a special form of _____ in which we think of the scenes of Jesus' suffering and death.

8. The Stations of the Cross are _____ or pictures of scenes of Jesus' death.

9. Jesus taught the _____ to pray.

Advent

apostles

children

colors

Cross

holy

home

meditation

peace

praise

prayers

public

statues

year

end

Glossary

absolution A blessing given as a sign of God's forgiveness.

Act of Contrition A prayer of sorrow for sins.

Acts of the Apostles The book of the New Testament that tells the story of the apostles and the Church after Jesus ascended to heaven.

adoration, adore Telling God how great he is and how much we need him.

adultery Being unfaithful to marriage vows.

Advent Four week season when we prepare for Christmas.

angels Spirits made by God to live in heaven and to be messengers and guardians.

Anointing of the Sick Sacrament in which God may bring healing to the sick.

Apostles Twelve men who were the closest followers of Jesus.

Baptism The first sacrament, a sacrament of initiation. The minister of Baptism pours water, and a person becomes a child of God, a member of the Church, and is freed from original sin.

Beatitudes Eight ways Jesus told us would make us blessed or happy. They are found in Matthew 5.

Bible A collection of books that are the Word of God. The Bible is divided into two sections: the Old Testament and the New Testament.

bishop A priest who receives the highest degree of Holy Orders so he can lead an area of the Church called a diocese. The twelve apostles were the first bishops of the Church.

Blessed Sacrament Another name for the Eucharist, the Body and Blood of Christ.

character A permanent spiritual sign. At both Baptism and Confirmation, we receive a special character, so these sacraments cannot be repeated.

Church The People of God who follow Jesus. The Church is one, holy, catholic, and apostolic.

communal Penance service A public gathering to celebrate the sacrament of Reconciliation with prayers and songs together, and private confession of sins.

confessional A room where we kneel to tell our sins to a priest during the sacrament of Reconciliation. (See also, reconciliation room.)

Confirmation Sacrament by which God gives us the gifts of the Holy Spirit.

Glossary

conscience The power inside each person to know what is right and what is wrong.

consecrate Pray the words that change the bread and wine into the Body and Blood of Christ.

corporal works of mercy List of seven ways we are called by Jesus to help others in a material way.

covenant Special promise between God and his people.

covet To want something that does not belong to you.

create To make something out of nothing.

creed A statement of what we believe.

deacon A man ordained to the third degree of Holy Orders to be of special service to the Church.

diaconate The third degree of Holy Orders, which ordains a man a deacon.

diocese A group of parishes in one area, led by a bishop.

Easter The feast of Jesus' Resurrection.

Epiphany The feast during the Christmas season when we commemorate the coming of the three wise men from the East to visit the child Jesus.

Eucharist The sacrament of bread and wine that becomes the sacrament of the Body and Blood of Jesus Christ.

Eucharistic minister The person who helps the priest distribute Communion at Mass.

faith The gift of believing in God and the Church.

Father The First Person in the Holy Trinity. The Father is God.

Good Friday The Friday in Holy Week when we commemorate Jesus' suffering and death.

Gospels The four books of the New Testament (Matthew, Mark, Luke, and John) that tell the story of Jesus' life.

grace God's life in our souls.

hallowed Holy.

holy Full of grace.

Holy Communion The Eucharist when we receive it at Mass.

Holy Family Jesus, his mother, Mary, and his foster father, Joseph.

Holy Orders Sacrament in which God gives the Church bishops, priests, and deacons.

Holy Spirit The Third Person in the Holy Trinity. The Holy Spirit is God.

Holy Thursday Thursday of Holy Week on which we commemorate the Last Supper Jesus ate with his apostles, the night he gave us his Body and Blood in the Eucharist.

Holy Trinity The name of the three persons in one God—the Father, the Son, and the Holy Spirit.

Immaculate Conception The mystery that teaches us Mary was without any sin from the first moment of her life.

inspire Put an idea or thought into someone's mind. God inspired the authors of the books of the Bible to write about him.

lector Person who reads the Word of God from Scripture to the assembly at liturgy.

Lent Forty days before Easter, when we remember how Jesus died on the cross.

liturgy The public worship of God.

Liturgy of the Eucharist The second part of the Mass, when the bread and wine become the Body and Blood of Christ.

Liturgy of the Word The first part of the Mass, when we hear the Word of the Lord from Scripture.

liturgical year The Church's marking of the year into seasons that remember the life of Christ and his Church.

Mass The special meal and sacrifice when bread and wine become the Body and Blood of Jesus Christ; the celebration of the Eucharist.

Matrimony Sacrament in which a man and woman become husband and wife in Christ.

meditation Prayer of thinking about Jesus or Mary and talking silently to God about how we can be more like them.

miracle An action done only through God's power. Jesus' greatest miracle was his rising from the dead.

moral decisions Choices between right and wrong.

mortal sin A very serious sin that cuts us off from God's life.

mystery of faith A teaching of our faith which we believe but cannot fully understand or explain.

New Testament The second section of the Bible, with 27 books written about Jesus and his Church.

obey Do what we are told to do.

Old Testament The first section of the Bible, with 46 books about God's chosen people.

original sin The first sin, when Adam and Eve did not obey God. Each person inherits this sin.

Palm Sunday The first day of Holy Week. We remember the day Jesus rode into Jerusalem while people welcomed him waving palm branches and shouting, "Hosanna!"

parables Stories that teach about God and his kingdom. Jesus told many parables.

parish A community of Catholic believers who gather in one church to worship and learn.

Glossary

pastor The leader of a parish.

paten Plate where the bread of Eucharist is placed at Mass.

patron saint A saint for whom someone is named or a saint who is prayed to for special reasons.

Penance Another name for the Sacrament of Reconciliation, the sacrament of forgiveness.

penance A prayer to say or an action to do to make up for sins.

Pentecost Sunday The day the Holy Spirit came upon the apostles. The "birthday of the Church."

pope The head of the Church on earth all over the world.

prayer The raising of one's mind and heart to God or the requesting of good things from God.

precepts of the Church Laws given by the Church to help us make moral decisions.

preside Serve as a leader. The priest presides or leads us at Mass.

priest A man ordained to the second degree of Holy Orders to celebrate Mass, forgive sins, and serve the Church as a teacher and leader.

profession of faith Statement of what we believe.

psalms Song prayers, especially the collection of these prayers found in the Book of Psalms in the Old Testament.

Reconciliation Sacrament in which Christ forgives sins.

reconciliation room Room where we may sit or kneel in private while we tell a priest our sins during the sacrament of Reconciliation.

Resurrection Jesus' greatest miracle, his rising from the dead.

reveal Let something be known. God reveals himself by letting us know about him.

Rosary Prayers to Mary prayed with a special set of beads to mark each Our Father, Hail Mary, and Doxology. While praying the prayers, we meditate on mysteries from the lives of Jesus and Mary.

Sabbath The Lord's Day, the seventh day when God rested after creating the world.

sacrament A sign of God's love, given to the Church by Jesus in which he gives us grace.

sacramental grace God's life given through any of the seven sacraments.

Sacramentary The book that contains the prayers for each liturgy.

sacraments of service The two sacraments that bless people for special tasks: Holy Orders and Matrimony.

sacraments of healing The two sacraments in which God gives healing: Reconciliation and Anointing of the Sick.

sacraments of initiation The three sacraments in which we become members of the Church: Baptism, Confirmation, and Eucharist.

sacrifice An offering to God to ask for special blessings.

saints Holy people who live with God in heaven.

Savior Someone who saves people or sets them free. Jesus is our Savior who freed us from sin.

Son The Second Person in the Holy Trinity. The Son is God. Jesus is the Son of God.

soul The part of each person that will never die. The soul is a spirit and cannot be seen.

spiritual works of mercy List of seven ways we are called by Jesus to help others in a spiritual way.

Sunday The Lord's Day. Sunday is special because Jesus rose from the dead on a Sunday.

Ten Commandments Laws or rules that show us how to love God and other people.

venial sin A less serious sin that does not cut us off from God's life but does weaken us spiritually.

wedding The ceremony of Matrimony, when a man and woman become husband and wife.

witness Someone who has seen an event and can tell what happened. There must be witnesses at each wedding.

Saints

Saints have come in all shapes, sizes, and races. They have been rich and poor, young and old. Some have been married and some have not. Some of them led very holy lives from childhood. Others had their lives changed in miraculous ways. They all have had in common a love for God and their neighbor.

St. Anthony

Feast day January 17

Just as you may have many friends with the same first name, the Church has many saints who had the same first name. We have several saints named Anthony, which can also be spelled A-N-T-O-N-Y. This particular Anthony is sometimes called "St. Anthony, the Abbot" because of how he lived his life. He came from the city of Koman in Egypt. So some people call him "St. Anthony of Koman." No matter how we refer to him, he is truly an extraordinary saint. Back in the old days, about 200 years after Jesus rose from the dead, Anthony gave up all his wealth and property. He did this so that he could spend all his time in prayer and penance. He ate only bread and water once a day. Yet Anthony was noted for his humility, joy, holiness, and wise leadership.

Do you think you could be happy eating only bread and water?

St. Thomas Aquinas

January 28

St. Thomas was a large man. He was a very good student but not very talkative. His classmates often teased him. They called him "the dumb ox." Thomas' family was wealthy and wanted him to join an order of priests where he would have power and prestige. Thomas chose to join the Dominicans, an order his family considered to be poor. St. Thomas is famous for a five-volume book called the *Summa Theologica*. Even though people praised Thomas for his intelligence, he was always quick to recognize it as a great gift from God.

Has anyone ever made fun of you? What did you do about it?

St. Louise de Marillac

Feast day March 15—Canonized 1934

Louise lost both of her parents before she was sixteen years old. She had a good education, was married, and had one child. However, her husband died after a long illness. Tragedy could not stop Louise from living a life of love and care. She was the good friend of a priest named Vincent de Paul. He helped her to see God's presence in her life. He is also a saint. He worked with poor people and asked Louise to help him. She not only helped but also taught other women how to help the poor and ill. Together St. Louise and St. Vincent began a religious order known as the Sisters of Charity. We call them the founders of the order.

Do you have a friend who helps you know God better?

St. George

April 23

St. George is a person who lived a very long time ago. We believe that he was a soldier who lived his faith with courage. He was so brave that he died rather than deny his faith. Emperor Diocletian had him beheaded. Devotion to St. George began very early. People told stories about St. George killing a dragon to save a town. When the king offered him a reward, he only asked that the king build churches, care for the poor, and help priests. Thus, St. George has been considered a model for all brave and humble Christians. King Richard I of England had a special devotion to St. George and declared him the patron of England. The stories people told about St. George may not be true, but his love for God and willingness to face death rather than deny his faith are truly heroic.

Who is your hero or heroine?

Saints

St. Jerome

Feast day September 30
Patron of Scripture scholars, librarians, and students

St. Jerome lived about 300 years after Jesus rose from the dead. He was born in a country called Dalmatia, now Yugoslavia. He was a very good student and wanted to spend his entire life in study. He was called, however, to serve as a priest and later became an advisor to the pope. In Jerome's lifetime, Latin was the main language of the people. The Bible was originally written in Hebrew and Greek. This was long before the printing press, so Bibles were very few in number, and each one was handwritten. Jerome knew that a Latin translation of the Bible would be important to the people. He used his knowledge to perform that translation. It took him over thirty years to complete the task. This Bible translation is called the Vulgate and was the official translation for many years.

How can you use your skills to help someone else?

Blessed Junipero Serra

Feast day July 1

Jose Miguel Serra was born in Spain. He joined the Franciscan religious order as a young man. Though his health was frail, he was a good preacher and asked to be a missionary. In the mid-1700's he sailed to Mexico. It was a terrible journey. They lacked food and water and experienced frightening storms. While in Mexico, Father Serra was bitten by an insect. The bite permanently damaged his leg. Though he was in constant pain, he continued to do God's work among the people of the area. Throughout his lifetime, he traveled up the coast of California building a total of nine missions to serve the people. He loved the Indian people and they loved him.

Have you ever been in pain? Who helped you?

St. Francis Xavier

Feast day December 3

Francis was born when his six brothers and sisters were much older. So he grew up almost like an only child. He was a great athlete and a good student. He was bright and generous. His early life was filled with luxury, pleasure, and fame. It was only later, after he met St. Ignatius of Loyola, that he knew his life was meant for greater things. Francis eventually became a priest in the religious order founded by St. Ignatius. He traveled to India to teach the children and help the sick and the poor. He later traveled to other countries and converted many people to Catholicism. We still have many of the letters he wrote to friends while he served in other countries. Sometimes we call St. Francis Xavier "the Apostle of the Indies."

Who challenges you to be the best person you can be?

St. Helen

Feast day August 18

St. Helen was a very holy woman who lived about 250 years after Jesus was raised from the dead. Helen was a married woman. She had a son named Constantine. He became a famous emperor. Most of her life, Helen was not a Christian. Her son Constantine was impressed by Christian teachings. He became the first Christian emperor and made it legal to be Christian. Helen was baptized when she was about sixty-three years old. She used her money and influence to help the poor. When she was eighty, her son Constantine asked her to oversee the building of a church on Golgotha, where Jesus had died. An ancient Church tradition states that St. Helen found the cross on which Jesus had been crucified. This tradition is not historically proven, but we do know that St. Helen had a special devotion to the cross of Jesus.

Do you know any person that helps you love Jesus more?

Sacred Sites

Sacred Sites are places you may visit, or think about, to help you get to know Jesus better.

Tabernacle

By now you know that the tabernacle is the place in a church where we keep the consecrated hosts that have not been used during Mass. Tabernacles come in many shapes and sizes. They are made of very solid materials. This is to protect the Blessed Sacrament from any harm.

Many years ago, all the bread that was consecrated at Mass had to be consumed. This meant that people who were very sick or very old, who could not get to Mass, could not receive Communion. The leaders of the Church knew that receiving Our Lord in the Eucharist could be very helpful to these people. They saw to it that any left-over consecrated bread would be stored with honor and care. This could then be taken to the sick and elderly.

Where is the tabernacle located in your church?

Hospitals

Hospitals are very sacred places. Doctors, nurses, janitors, secretaries, and all people who work in hospitals have a very sacred job. They help to comfort and care for people who are ill. You have probably heard the many stories about Jesus curing those who were ill. People who work in hospitals are doing what Jesus would do. They are very special to Jesus.

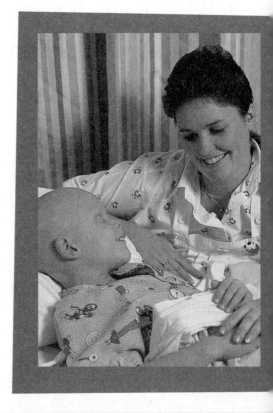

Hospitals are sacred for another reason. The people who are ill are also very special to Jesus. During his life, Jesus often spent time with those who were ill, in pain, or dying. He took time to be with people who had a terrible skin disease called leprosy. He healed people who had terrible fevers. He raised up a little girl who was in a coma. He healed a lady who was bleeding very badly. Jesus loved those who were suffering.

Who takes care of you when you are ill?

Homeless Shelters

Earlier in this book, you read about the corporal and spiritual works of mercy. Those who serve in homeless shelters are doing most, if not all, of those works of mercy. It is obvious that they provide food, drink, clothing, and shelter to those in need. They are often asked to find assistance for those who are ill or just released from prison. On occasion, they must arrange to bury someone who has died with no family to care for him or her.

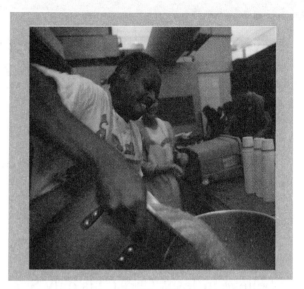

We must remember that every person, rich or poor, healthy or ill, saint or sinner is created and cherished by God. Jesus told us that whenever we care for someone in need we are actually taking care of him. The people who need to use homeless shelters are the people that God gives us to help us find our way to him. Mother Teresa of Calcutta was a very holy woman who worked with homeless people. She always said that when she cared for one of these she was caring for Jesus himself.

How could your family help a homeless shelter in your area?

Jordan River

Jesus had an older cousin named John, the son of Elizabeth and Zechariah. When John was a young man, he went out to the desert to pray. God revealed to him that the Messiah was soon to come. John came out of the desert and began to speak to the people near the Jordan River. John began telling the people they needed to change their lives. He had a strong message.

One day, John saw another young man coming toward him. God let John know that this man, his cousin Jesus, was the promised Messiah. Jesus asked John to baptize him. John said to Jesus, "I should be baptized by you." But Jesus insisted and was baptized in the waters of the Jordan River.

Where were you baptized?

Prayers are the ways we communicate with God. When we pray, we talk to God and we also listen for guidance.

Prayers of the Rosary

Sign of the Cross

In the name of the Father, and of the Son, and of the Holy Spirit, Amen.

Apostles' Creed

I believe in God, the Father Almighty,
    creator of heaven and earth.
I believe in Jesus Christ, his only Son, our Lord.
        He was conceived by the power of the Holy Spirit
            and born of the Virgin Mary.
        He suffered under Pontius Pilate,
            was crucified, died and was buried.
        He descended to the dead.
        On the third day he rose again.
        He ascended into heaven
            and is seated at the right hand of the Father.
        He will come again to judge the living and the dead.
I believe in the Holy Spirit,
        the holy catholic church,
        the communion of saints,
        the forgiveness of sins,
        the resurrection of the body,
        and life everlasting. Amen.

Our Father

Our Father, who art in heaven,
hallowed be thy name;
thy Kingdom come;
thy will be done on earth as it is in heaven.
Give us this day our daily bread;
and forgive us our trespasses
as we forgive those who trespass against us;
and lead us not into temptation,
but deliver us from evil. Amen.

Hail Mary

Hail Mary, full of grace, the Lord is with you.
Blessed are you among women,
and blessed is the fruit of your womb, Jesus.
Holy Mary, Mother of God,
pray for us sinners
now and at the hour of our death. Amen.

Doxology

Glory to the Father, and to the Son,
and to the Holy Spirit: as it was in the beginning,
is now, and will be for ever. Amen.

A Few More Special Prayers...

Prayer to Your Guardian Angel

Angel of God, my guardian dear,
To whom God's love entrusts me here.
Ever this day be at my side,
To light and guard, to rule and guide. Amen.

An Act of Contrition

My God,
I am sorry for my sins with all my heart.
In choosing to do wrong
and failing to do good,
I have sinned against you
whom I should love above all things.
I firmly intend, with your help,
to do penance,
to sin no more,
and to avoid whatever leads me to sin.
Our Savior Jesus Christ
suffered and died for us.
In his name, my God, have mercy. Amen.

Come Holy Spirit

Come, Holy Spirit, fill the hearts of your faithful.
And kindle in them the fire of your love.
Send forth your Spirit and they shall be created.
And you will renew the face of the earth.
Let us pray.
Lord,
by the light of the Holy Spirit
you have taught the hearts of your faithful.
In the same Spirit
help us to relish what is right
and always rejoice in your consolation.
We ask this through Christ our Lord. Amen.

Grace Before Meals

Bless us, O Lord, and these your gifts
which we are about to receive from your goodness.
Through Christ our Lord. Amen.

We go to Mass each week and on special holy days.

Every day of the year, except Good Friday, Mass is offered. This is the opportunity for us to receive Jesus into our hearts. Some people are very fortunate and can attend Mass every day at their parish. In some small parishes, Mass is only offered on the weekends. But for all of us Catholics, it is a rule of the Church that we participate in Mass every weekend and on special holy days. It is one of the ways that we honor the Third Commandment and keep holy the Sabbath. When we miss Mass on a Sunday because we were lazy or tired, we commit a serious sin and should go to confession before we receive Holy Communion again.

Do you remember what these rules of the Church are called?

We end our prayers with the word Amen.

Amen is a very special word. It is used often during Mass and generally when we end a prayer. It is a very old word that means "Yes" or "So be it." It shows that we agree with everything that was just said in the prayer. We respond, "Amen," to the words "Body of Christ" just before we receive Holy Communion,

We are saying, "Yes, I believe this is really Jesus I am about to receive."

We use a monstrance.

A monstrance is a sacred vessel that allows the consecrated host to be shown outside of Mass during a ceremony called Adoration of the Blessed Sacrament.

Monstrances come in various shapes and sizes. Some are very simple, while others can be very fancy. Others even have precious jewels on them. A very common form is a shape that reminds us of the sun. The host is visible in a glass container in the center of the sun shape. The glass container at the center is removable and is called a lunula, luna, or lunette.

Does your parish have a monstrance? Ask your parish priest.

The celebrant at Adoration uses a humeral veil.

All our actions during Adoration of the Blessed Sacrament help us to remember how sacred the host is. After all, it is the Body of Jesus. During Adoration, the celebrant holds up the monstrance with the Blessed Sacrament in it and blesses the people. This is called Benediction. The celebrant covers his hands with a long rectangular cloth before he touches the monstrance that holds the consecrated host. This very fancy cloth is called a humeral veil.

Have you attended Adoration of the Blessed Sacrament at your church?

We sign ourselves at the reading of the Gospel.

At Mass, just before the reading of the Gospel, the priest or deacon says, "A reading from the Gospel according to...". Then he names one of the four Gospels: Matthew, Mark, Luke, or John. We respond, "Glory to you, O Lord." While we say these words, we reverently trace the Sign of the Cross, using our right thumb, over our forehead, lips, and heart. This sign expresses our prayer that the Word of God might be always in our mind, on our lips, and in our heart. What a wonderful way to prepare ourselves to listen to God's Good News!

Can you make this wonderful prayer movement?

Answer Key

Lesson 1 Activity:
1. gift
2. faith
3. three persons
4. God, holy

Message: There is one God

Lesson 2 Activity
Drawings will vary.

Lesson 3 Activity
Message: I will send a Savior.

Lesson 4 Activity

Hidden message: Jesus is God the Father's promise.

Lesson 5 Activity
1. went to the desert to pray.
2. had twelve apostles.
3. worked miracles.
4. is our Savior.

Lesson 6 Activity

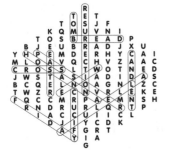

Lesson 7 Activity

Lesson 8 Activity
Saints are good and faithful people.
They live in heaven with God.

Section One Review
1. faith
2. persons
3. mystery
4. nothing
5. image
6. will
7. original
8. Satan
9. Savior
10. four
11. miracle
12. Mary
13. heaven

Lesson 9 Activity
1. new life
2. Spirit
3. holy food
4. no sin
5. healing
6. service
7. faithful

Lesson 10 Activity
1. initiation, grace, members, Church
2. Oil, water
3. Holy Spirit, water
4. Holy Spirit, oil
5. once, souls, character

Lesson 11 Activity
"In memory…" — meal

"Lord God…" — sacrifice

"Through your goodness…" — meal

"Happy are those…" — meal

"Bless and approve…" — sacrifice

"Let it become for us…" — sacrifice

"You have gathered us…" — meal

Lesson 12 Activity
Bishop, Priest, Deacon

Lesson 13 Activity
1. promises
2. grace
3. faithful
4. children
5. lives
6. home
7. together
8. loving
9. family

Lesson 14 Activity
Drawings will vary.

Lesson 15 Activity

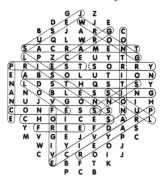

Section Two Review
1. life
2. Baptism, Eucharist, Confirmation
3. meal, sacrifice
4. Body, Blood, Eucharist
5. Bishop
6. vows
7. heal
8. absolution

Lesson 16 Activity
1. George: virtue
2. Mandy: sin
3. David: sin
4. Nathan: sin
5. Barbara: virtue
6. Steve: virtue
7. Jason: virtue
8. Juanita: sin
9. Judy: sin
10. Jim: virtue

Lesson 17 Activity
false, #8

true, #4

false, #6

false, #7

true, #1

false, #5

true, #2

true, #3

Lesson 18 Activity
Shelter the homeless.

Pray for the living and the dead.

Instruct the ignorant.

Feed the hungry.

Warn the sinner.

Give drink to the thirsty.

Clothe the naked.

Lesson 19 Activity

Lesson 20 Activity
Left column

2 You shall not take the name of the Lord your God in vain.

3 Remember to keep holy the Lord's Day.

1 I am the Lord your God; you shall not have strange gods before me.

Right column

4 Honor your father and your mother.

9 You shall not covet your neighbor's wife.

6 You shall not commit adultery.

7 You shall not steal.

5 You shall not kill.

10 You shall not covet anything that belongs to your neighbor.

8 You shall not bear false witness against your neighbor.

Lesson 21 Activity
1. one, have
2. first, people
3. good, all
4. God, name
5. holy

Transfer message: Love and honor God.

Lesson 22 Activity
Answers will vary.

Lesson 23 Activity
1. Children, obey, parents
2. children. everyone
3. Jesus, obey, laws
4. love, parents, respect
5. respect, obey, teachers, leaders.

Answer Key

Lesson 24 Activity
I have set before you life and death…

Choose life!

Lesson 25 Activity

Lesson 26 Activity
1. breaking, 10
2. keeping 7
3. keeping 7
4. keeping 10
5. breaking 7
6. keeping 7

Lesson 27 Activity

Section Three Review
1. conscience, decide
2. free, choices
3. away
4. Mortal. Venial
5. happy
6. material
7. Church
8. life, God
9. image
10. covet
11. property

Lesson 28 Activity
David

Moses

Catholics

Jesus

Joseph and Mary

Abraham and Sarah

Jewish

Lesson 29 Activity

Message: Liturgy is public worship.

Lesson 30 Activity
1. contrition
2. asking
3. contrition
4. adoration
5. praise
6. thanks
7. asking

Lesson 31 Activity
Drawings will vary.

Lesson 32 Activity
1. d
2. b
3. e
4. a
5. f
6. c
7. g

Section Four Review
1. public
2. home, prayers
3. year
4. Advent
5. meditation
6. praise
7. Cross, meditation
8. statues
9. apostles